Anonymous

Polk Benton Harbor-St. Joseph

Michigan City Directory

Anonymous

Polk Benton Harbor-St. Joseph
Michigan City Directory

ISBN/EAN: 9783744760362

Printed in Europe, USA, Canada, Australia, Japan

Cover: Foto ©ninafisch / pixelio.de

More available books at **www.hansebooks.com**

ROLLINS

PUBLISHING COMPANY'S

ST. JOSEPH

AND

BENTON HARBOR

DIRECTORY,

Containing Historical and Descriptive Sketches of both places, and a full list of the Residents, together with a Business Directory, and a full record of Fruit Growers and Shippers.

CHICAGO:
ROLLINS PUBLISHING COMPANY.
161 LASALLE STREET.
1878.

ST. JOSEPH.

DESCRIPTIVE.

St. Joseph, one of the most important commercial points in the state of Michigan, and as well one of the most attractive summer resorts of the lake region, is situated at the mouth of the St. Joseph river, on Lake Michigan in latitude 42 degrees north. Placed upon nearly the same parallel with Boston, the climate of St. Joseph and its neighborhood is much more mild and equable than that of New England, or any part of the north Atlantic coast, owing to causes of a local character. It is distant from Chicago sixty-two miles, from Racine seventy-five miles, and from Milwaukee one hundred miles. With all of these, and other prominent over-lake ports, daily steamer communication is maintained during the entire season of navigation. Ample rail communication with all christendom is also enjoyed by means of the facilities furnished by the Chicago and Michigan Lake Shore Railway.

The county is traversed by the St. Joseph river, from the south-east, passing through the city of Niles and the villages of Buchanan and Berrien; the Paw Paw river crosses it from the north-east, flowing through the village of Watervliet and not far from Coloma. Near the mouth of the former the two rivers unite, forming, with the lake, two peninsulas. Steamer navigation is practicable on the St. Joseph river for a distance of one hundred miles from its mouth, and on the Paw Paw for about thirty miles. The Harbor of St. Joseph is one of the finest in the state, and it

lacks nothing to make it one of the best on the great lakes, but the expenditure of a moderate sum of money, which it is believed the general government will soon see the justice and expediency of appropriating, in view of the already considerable and rapidly accreting commercial importance of the place.

The beautiful village of St. Joseph is located upon a plateau fifty feet above the level of the lake and river, and on the peninsula between those waters. The site, whether considered from the practical or æsthetic point of view, is one of the most attractive in the northwest, combining as it does, all the advantages of situation necessary for the material well being of a thriving manufacturing and trading town, with the charms of rare scenery and delightful surroundings. To the sportsman, the locality offers an additional attraction, in being one of the finest and most accessible fishing and shooting grounds in the country. Without aspiring to the possession of immense public edifices, like the great cities, St. Joseph's citisens have nevertheless displayed a public spirit in this direction, of which much larger and more pretentious towns might well be proud. Among the prominent buildings of the village a substantial and handsome Union School, enjoying merited prosperity, is especially noticable. There are, also. several churches, four of which are attractive and commodious brick structures ; and one of these, the M. E. Church edifice, is acknowledged to be one of the finest in the state, west of Detroit.

At the present time the population of St. Joseph is about 3.000, a noticable gain since the date of the last census, which placed it at 2,718. The township is a small one geographically speaking, as it contains only seven sections of land, some portions of which are at present uninhabited owing to the swampy nature of the ground. In 1864 the population was only 1,681, which number has been increased to about 3,500, that figuring closely approximate the present number of inhabitants.

The soil of the neighborhood is extremely fertile, consisting of a rich sandy loam, with occasional clay outcroppings. Formerly it was heavily timbered, having been well covered with oak, and less generally, but to a considerable extent, in places, with maple, beech, whitewood, black walnut, ash, butternut, hickory, together with some pine. The land in this locality is eminently adapted to successful agriculture, and yields prolific crops of the cereals and

other products common to favored sections of the temperate zone. The wheat grown in the country is not excelled in the west. But since Nature has specially endowed this part of her garden with a golden capability to produce the most delicious fruits of the plant, vine, and tree, in such excellence and abundance as to supply the markets of Michigan, Illinois, Wisconsin, and other Western states, the ordinary avocations of the farm have been to a great extent abandoned "for the more glorious purpose," as the Free Masons say, of fruit growing; hence fruit is the principal export of St. Joseph, and the basis of many of its most successful manufactures.

The neighborhood of St. Joseph has the deserved reputation of being the best fruit growing region in the north-west. In the autumn the prevailing lake winds check the growth of the trees, in consequence of which their wood is more thoroughly matured than would otherwise happen, and they are in better condition to resist the attacks of winter storms and frosts. Again, during the coldest season of the year, the winds blowing from over the open waters of Lake Michigan, which are far milder than those which sweep over frost bound and snow covered regions, so modify the climate, that the thermometer very rarely registers a temperature below zero. If we wanted to ascend into the realm of poetry, we might excusably call St. Joseph "the child of the Lake Wind," for its benefits and support come largely from that important influence, whose benignity lasts the year around. Again in the spring its helpful presence is felt, when by its aid the fruit trees' growth is retarded, and the fruit thus insured against destruction by late frosts. The environment of the vicinity also, in respect of the lake and rivers, is an additional protection against the frosts of spring. So mild indeed is the climate of this enviable place, that garden vegetables frequently remain green until the first of December.

HISTORICAL.

Prior to the year 1822, the valley of the St. Joseph was a wilderness, and from one end to the other, without a white settler. In the year named, Rev. Isaac McCoy, a Baptist missionary, established a mission, one mile east of the place where the present city of Niles is located. This enterprise was under the denominational board of missions, who christened it the "Carey Mission," in

honor of a noted missionary to India, of their faith. At this time there were a few half-breeds at St. Joseph, and Pere Aux Vaches, who traded with the Indians and cultivated a few patches of ground; otherwise the nomadic red-man was the sole occupant of the entire region.

Properly speaking, the settlement of St. Joseph dates from the year 1829. In 1828 a treaty was made, at Carey mission, with the Pottawotomie Indians, by which they ceded to the United States, a considerable tract of land, a portion of which is now known as Berrien County. Calvin Britain and Augustus P. Newell pre-empted the land upon which the village of St. Joseph now stands, in 1829. These lands were surveyed by the government in the following year, and were purchased by the pre-empters. Major Britain laid the village out in 1831, and March 7, 1834, it was incorporated by act of the territorial legislature, as the village of St. Joseph; although when first laid out, it had been called Newburyport.

Of the early settlers—those who came here prior to 1830—very few are known to be living, and of these, the larger proportion still cling to the scenes and associations of their early pioneer days. In 1831, the first marriage occurred in the little community, and Mr. Bartlett was joined in wedlock to Miss Pamelia Ives. The first white child born in the settlement, came to this couple in the person of Calvin Bartlett, now living and known as one of the most popular steamboat captains on the lakes. The first warehouse, a log structure, was erected by Amos B. Hinckley, in 1830. The first saw mill was started two years later by Deacon & McKaleb; it stood about midway between the foot of Main street and the bayou bridge. The first steamboat whose paddles ever scared the fish in the St. Joseph river, was built by the same parties in 1833, and called the Matilda Barney; its first commander was Captain Daniel Wilson. A. E. Draper edited and published the first newspaper, the *St. Joseph Herald*, in 1833, but the venture was not a paying one, and was abandoned before long.

In 1836, under an appropriation made under General Jackson's administration, work was commenced on the harbor piers. Before the piers were built and the channel of the river changed, the mouth of the St. Joseph was opposite the lighthouse. At that time it was a difficult river to enter, especially in rough weather,

and many valuable lives had been lost in the attempt before the present harbor protections were constructed. In 1831 the old lighthouse was commenced; the keeper's house occupied the site, of the present one, and the tower was on the brow of the hill in front of it.

From the time of its settlement up to 1846 St. Joseph increased rapidly in population and business importance, and a considerable trade was established between the village and river points as far up as Three Rivers, and Chicago. The trade with the latter, indeed, was important enough to employ several large steamers. In those days it was the intention of the state government to make St. Joseph the terminus of the Michigan Central Railroad, and this prospective aggrandisement for the town had the effect of starting a wild speculation in real estate, which was held at enormous prices, much to the detriment of solid prosperity and normal progress. The sale of the Central road by the state to the Michigan Central Railroad Company, practically put a period to these ambitious anticipations, for, although in the original draft of the charter, the company was obliged to make its terminus at St. Joseph, by representing that it might find it more to its advantage to make it at South Haven or at some point farther north, the charter was amended so as to oblige the company to build their road to some point in the state on Lake Michigan feasible for steamboats. Mr. Brooks the astute manager of the road complied with the requirements of the charter by building the line to New Buffalo, where a temporary harbor "feasible for steamboats" was constructed at considerable expense; but this was allowed to go to decay and the road was continued around the head of the lake to Chicago. By this sharp, though perhaps questionable move, Chicago gained one of her most important railway connections and St. Joseph lost the opportunity of becoming one of the great cities of the West, at least for the succeeding generation or so. What the future may have in store for it as a result of the steadily growing importance of its valuable productions, trade, and manufactures, is yet to be seen. One thing is very certain that at present St. Joseph is only second to Detroit in commercial importance in the state, and its prosperity stands upon the most solid foundation.

BUSINESS ENTERPRISES.

It may not be improper in a work of this kind to give a brief description of persons, firms and corporations upon the results of whose enterprise the wealth and standing of St. Joseph rests. It may be further remarked *en passant* that among the professional and busines men of the town, not a few are notables of more than local reputation in the fields of commerce, politics and the arts and sciences.

Among the leading men not only of St. Joseph, but of the State of Michigan, one man is noteworthy as being an influence to which his section stands indebted for much of its later progress and wealth. Since the sketch of the gentleman we refer to in the history of Michigan could not be improved upon by us, we reproduce it:

"Alexander Hamilton Morrison, of St. Joseph, Michigan, projector and builder of the Michigan Lake Shore Railroad and its vice-president and general manager, was born in the Province of Quebec, Canada, February 22, 1822. At the age of fifteen he was engaged as clerk for B. W. Smith, now sheriff of Simcoe, Ontario, and with him came West in 1838, arriving at Chicago in October of that year, when Chicago contained less than four thousand inhabitants. Here he entered the employ of David Ballentine, Esq., then a contractor on the Illinois and Michigan canal and remained with him as clerk for several years. At the age of nineteen he engaged in active business on his own account. In 1847, 1848 and 1849 Mr. Morrison was engaged as a contractor on public works in Illinois and Iowa. In 1850 he came to St. Joseph, where he has since resided and has been connected in extensive business as a merchant and lumberman, until he engaged in the railroad enterprise which now occupies his attention.

The Chicago and Michigan Lake Shore Railroad, of which Mr. Morrison is the projector, builder and successful general manager extends from New Buffalo on the Michigan Central to Pentwater, which is the main line, a distance of one hundred and seventy miles, with a branch of twenty miles from Holland to Grand Rapids and another branch from Muskegon to Big Rapids of fifty-five miles, making in all two hundred and fifty miles of road. Con-

sidering the difficulties encountered in consequence of the decision of the Supreme court declaring void all municipal aid voted to help construct railways together with the fact that the road was built through a new country sparsely populated and which would not have been undertaken without the encouragement the law of 1869, opposed the success of the enterprise in both its completion and management entitles to the projector and builder to an amount of praise for commercial sagacity, foresight and economy in all the details of construction and management seldom awarded to men of these times, and which to him in his declining years will be a great source of consolation and pride. Mr. Morrison while engaged in extensive business has at the same time given some attention to politics and been the recipient of political honors and seen much of public life for a man of his years, now only fifty-two. In 1851 he was chairman of the board of supervisors of Berrien county. In 1852 he was a candidate for presidential elector on the Whig ticket. In 1856 he was elected to the Senate of this State. In 1860 he was elected to the House of Representatives, and was chairman of the committee on state affairs for three sessions and during that time was one of the special joint committee on war matters of which Hons. Jas. F. Joy, H. P. Baldwin and Thomas D. Gilbert, were members. To the members of that committee must be awarded the honor of successfully projecting that policy which at the end of the war found the State unincumbered with a war debt. The individual members of that committee were also foremost in sustaining a policy not less important, inaugurated by Mr. Joy at the first session of the Legislature of 1861, for the establishment of a sinking fund which in 1881 will find the state entirely out of debt. In 1862 Mr. Morrison was appointed by President Lincoln collector of internal revenue for the Second district of Michigan, and 1867 assessor of internal revenue for the same district which office he held until June 1869, when he resigned to enter upon the railroad project of which mention is made above. Mr. Morrison belongs to one of the pioneer families of the Western country, who were Indian traders in the Lake Superior country in the latter part of last century, and the first part of this. His father was a member of the old Northwestern Fur Company, and one of the few partners in that company that refused to surrender to and successfully resisted Lord Selkirk in his war made upon it

in the interest of the Hudson Bay Company, immediately after the late war with great Britain. His guardian in his boyhood and under whose care he was educated was his friend and relative the late William Morrison, the discoverer of the source of the Mississippi river, from whom he obtained a knowledge of pioneer life in the beginning of this century by hearing him relate adventures that, to the young, have a charm that is irresistible. Mr. Morrison ascribes his late success to his business connection with the Hon. James F. Joy, the great railroad magnate of the Northwest, to whom he always gives the entire praise. Be that as it may the people of Michigan will always remember the subject of this sketch as one of her distinguished characters and the people of the town of St. Joseph and Berrien county as its most prominent, widely known and ambitious business man, who for nearly twenty-five years has maintained a spotless reputation as a merchant and railroad manager."

One of the most prosperous financial institutions in western Michigan is the First National Bank of St. Joseph, which was organized in 1871, with a cash capital of $50,000. This bank transacts a large business with fruit growers, manufacturers and merchants and with their connections in Chicago and other markets. It is a great convenience, especially to Chicago commission merchants, who save a great deal of trouble and expense by transacting their business through this institution. The officers are W. E. Higman, president; James Baley, cashier, and O. O. Jordan, assistant cashier.

The carriage and wagon factory of Sam Hannon, on State street, is a prominent and successful manufacturing enterprise. The proprietor has established a reputation for making durable, strong and elegant wagons and carriages of all descriptions, and has established a large trade with the surrounding country, and other parts of the state as well as with more distant points.

Messrs Wallace & Barnes, on Water street at the foot of State, do an extensive business in lumber, lath, shingles, fencing, building material and so forth. They also deal largely in lime, salt, cement and land plaster. The house is well established and ranks high in its particular line among the leading firms of the section.

The news of the day is furnished to the people of St. Joseph by the *St. Joseph Republican*, an excellent weekly democratic paper

published by Wm. Ricaby & Son, No. 44 State street. The *Republican* is widely circulated in Berrien and adjacent counties and is a well conducted and ably edited journal. A first class job office with all the necessary facilities for a large business is attached to to the paper.

The stove, tinware, copper and sheet iron ware establishment of Charles H. Moulton, No. 42 State street, supplies the town and country about to a large extent. Mr. Moulton is a successful merchant, and has a business that is growing rapidly in volume and profit.

The leading drug and grocery house of the village is owned and managed by E. Palmer at Nos. 44 and 46 State street, who also keeps a heavy stock of wall papers. The business of this house is large and increasing with the growth of the locality.

The leading livery and sale stable of St. Joseph is the establishment of J. C. Caldwell, on State street, south of Broad and opposite the Park Hotel. Mr. Caldwell owns a number of fine carriage and draught horses and furnishes teams and carriages at the shortest notice. This stable is well known and popular, and deserves an excellent run of custom from citizens and visitors.

William Ricaby, in addition to his connection with the *Republican* conducts the largest business in St. Joseph in the line of watches, jewelry, books, stationery, music, musical instruments, fancy goods, etc., No. 48 State street, corner Pleasant. This house carries a large, varied and elegant stock of everything included in the above branches, and is a museum of *bijouterie* music, art and literature.

Frederick Sauerbier has a large grocery and provision house on Main street, and deals in choice family groceries, provisions, crockery, woodware, green and dried fruits, &c., &c.

C. C. Sweet & Bros., are the leading commercial firm of St. Joseph. They own and run an extensive general store at the corner of State and Ship streets and conduct one of the heaviest trading enterprises in this part of Michigan.

The most important manufacture of St. Joseph is that of fruit packages, to which business the labor and capital of several firms is devoted. Of the leading houses in this line, Messrs. A. W. Wells & Co., manufacture a vast amount of all kinds of fruit pack-

ages and have markets for their wares at home, in Chicago and other large cities. The firm composed is of young men, active energetic, enterprising and popular, is regarded as one of the most solid institutions of the town.

Another house in the same interest and equal to the first in commercial importance is the fruit package manufacturing establishment of Messrs. W. R. Wilcox & Co. This house has an extensive home trade and ships its product to all parts of the United States.

St. Joseph counts among its important industrial enterprises the extensive sash, door and blind factory of W. A. Preston, in connection with which there is a large planing mill. Mr. Preston enjoys a profitable trade, dealing heavily with his own people and surrounding counties and shipping to distant points to a considerable extent.

Among the leading members of the Michigan bar, the law firm of Potter & Potter, St. Joseph, are prominently known. Mr. C. B. Potter was democratic candidate for Congress during the last campaign, and made a fine run notwithstanding the fact that the district was overwhelmingly republican. The other notable counsellors of the locality are Messrs. Clapp & Fyfe, N. A. Hamilton and Thomas J. DePuy.

The medical profession is ably represented in the persons of Doctors A. K. Webster, A. H. Scott and L. J. McLin; and the leading dentist is Dr. H. C. Rockwell.

In respect of hotel facilities St. Joseph is far in advance of any town in Western Michigan. The leading house, the Park Hotel, is known everywhere as one of the most popular and comfortable resorts in the county. The buildings once constituted one of the handsomest private mansions in the state, and in the remodeling necessary for hotel purposes care was taken that the air of home comfort should not be lost. The grounds surrounding the house are beautifully laid out and are thoroughly shaded in summer by magnificent forest trees. The proprietor, Mr. Sam Brown is widely known as a genial and attentive host and the Park Hotel under his supervision has grown to be considered the ideal of a public house. The *cuisine* is unexceptionable, the rooms large, airy and furnished with taste and elegance, and the situation charming as to surroundings and central as to business requirements. Hundreds of sportsmen from the great cities make the Park Hotel their re-

sort during the fishing and shooting seasons, and it is needless to say that their every want is anticipated and provided for by this jolliest Boniface in Michigan—Sam Brown. There are several other hotels in St. Joseph of lesser note; they are the Guernsey, National and Hoyt houses.

CHICAGO AND MICHIGAN LAKE SHORE RAILROAD.

Almost, if not quite, first among the influences that unite to give St. Joseph, its neighboring town, Benton Horbor, and the locality generally, whatever of commercial advantage and prosperity now enjoyed by them, the railroad interest is worthy of attention. The great iron line which connects the section overland with Chicago and the other markets of the country, is the Chicago and Michigan Lake Shore Railroad, mention of which has been made elsewhere in connection with a sketch of the Hon. Alexander H. Morrison.

Its main line extends from New Buffalo to Pentwater, 170 miles, with a branch from Holland to Grand Rapids, 25 miles, and another from Muskegon to Big Rapids, 55 miles. Trains

section cut out of original

with sleeping coaches attached, run direct from Chicago via. this line to Grand Rapids, via. Holland. The distance from Chicago to New Buffalo is 66 miles, and from thence to Grand Rapids 115 miles. On the line of the road the points of greatest commercial importance are St. Joseph and Benton Harbor, in addition to which there are the thriving business and manufacturing towns of New Buffalo, Hartford, Bangor (where there are large furnaces and

..., Worcester, Alleyton, White Cloud, Traverse Road, Hungerford, and Big Rapids.

The equipment of the Chicago and Michigan Lake Shore Railroad is complete and ample; it has 250 flat cars, 150 box cars, 12 first-class passenger coaches, and 27 engines. The road is well graded, tied and ironed, and is regarded by experts to be in as satisfactory a condition as any line of railway in the country. Both its freight and passenger traffic are extensive and rapidly increasing under the energetic management of George C. Kimball, Esq., general manager, an officer whose executive abilities command for him the respect of the railroad profession, and of the public. Mr. Kimball's task is lightened by the assistance of an excellent staff. Mr. C. M. Lawler, assistant superintendent, is a

railroad official of high standing and ability, justly popular with the friends and patrons of the road. Mr. A. M. Nichols, general freight and passenger agent, is also a well-known, respected and able officer. The united labors of these gentlemen and of the other officers of the road have made the Chicago and Michigan Lake Shore Railroad an inconceivably great agent of prosperity for this part of the West, and in addition to that, one of the most important lines in the American system of railways.

Societies.

ST. JOSEPH COUNCIL, NO. 44, R. & S. M., A. F. & A. M.—Meets Monday evening after full moon. Officers, Alex. Elton, T. I. M.; J. W. Brewer, Recorder.

OCCIDENTAL LODGE, F. & A. M.—Meets at Masonic hall, Hoyt's brick block, on Thursday on or before full moon. Geo. S. Clapp, W. M. Chas. H. Moulton, Secretary.

CALVIN BRITAIN CHAPTER, R. A. M.—Meets Wednesday evening on or before full moon, at 7½ o'clock. H. M. Zekind, H. P., Law C. Fyfe, Secretary.

POMONA LODGE, F. & A. M. [281].—Regular meetings on Tuesday evenings on or before the full of the moon. John F. Gard, W. M. H. B., Enos, Secretary.

I. O. of O. F.—Barnett Lodge No. 119, Independent Order of Odd Fellows, hold its regular meetings at Odd Fellows' Hall, St. Joseph Mich., on Friday evening of each week. R. S. Hudson, N. G. J. A. Powell, Secretary.

ST. JOSEPH ENCAMPMENT NO. 37, I. O. O. F.—Regular meetings at Burnett hall, on the first and third Monday evenings of each month. O. D. Rector, C. P. S. Ritchie, Scribe.

YOUNG MEN'S CHRISTIAN ASSOCIATION.—Rooms in Palmer's Hall, nearly opposite Postoffice. Free reading room. All are cordially invited.

St. Joseph Churches.

METHODIST EPISCOPAL.—Rev. I. R. A. Wightman, pastor. Sunday services 10:30 A. M. and 7 P. M., Sabbath school after morning services. Prayer meeting, Thursday evening at 7 o'clock.

FIRST CONGREGATIONAL.—Rev. Abel S. Wood, pastor, Sunday services 10:30 A. M., and 7 P. M., Sabbath school after morning services. Prayer meeting Thursday evening 7 o'clock.

FIRST GERMAN BAPTIST.—Rev. D. Zwink, pastor. Services every Sunday 10:30 A. M., 7 P. M. Sabbath school, 2 P. M. Prayer meeting Wednesday, 7 P. M.

GERMAN LUTHERAN.—Rev. E. C. Georgii, pastor. Services Sunday at 10:30 A. M. Catechism in the afternoon at 2:30.

GERMAN EVANGELICAL.—Rev. C. Ude, pastor. Services at 10:30 A. M. Sunday school at 9 o'clock in the morning. Prayer meeting, Wednesday evening at 7½ o'clock.

CATHOLIC CHURCH.—Father Thiesen, pastor. Mass, 8 A. M.; second Mass 10:30 A. M.

St. Joseph Fire Co. No. 1.

Chief—T. T. Ransom.
Ass'ts—C. C. Sweet, E. C. Palmer.
Captain of Hose—Geo. W. Platt.
Secretary—H. C. Rockwell.
Treasurer—E. D. Crane.

Township Officers.

Supervisor—E. M. Edwards.
Town Clerk—W. H. Maynard.
Treasurer—Ed. F. Platt.
Commissioner of Highways—L. Collins.
Justices of the Peace—
    Jos. W. Brewer, term expires 1881.
    John Thomas, term expires 1880.
    Hiram Brown, term expires 1879.
    Daniel Chapman, term expires 1882.
School Inspector—Law C. Fyfe.
Superintendent Schools—R. F. Stratton.
Drain Commissioner—Samuel Reed.
Constables—Jos. J. Pearl, Jas. R. Clarke, F. Myer, W. C. Beyea.

Village Officers.

President—Geo. E. Smith.
Recorder—H. C. Rockwell.
Treasurer—John Martin.
Trustees—Ed. C. Palmer, A. B. Perkins, C. Kamerer, F. Sauerbier, J. A. Canavan.

ROLLINS PUBLISHING COMPANY'S

St. Joseph City Directory

FOR 1878-79.

Abbott E. L. res. Wayne.
Anderson Carl, res. Main.
Armstrong C. Miss, res. Park.
Armstrong S. M. res. Price.

Baldrey A. res. Broad.
Baldwin Judson, res. Court.
Ballard N. Mrs. res. State.
Barnes A. res. Ship.
Barnes M. C. res. State.
Bartlett Mrs. res. Front.
Bear Joseph, res. Church.
Beers A. J. res. Broad.
Benning Daniel, res. Main.
Benning H. res. Broad.
Benning J. res. Price.
Benning W. res. Wayne.

i

Bentley C. Mrs. res. Second Front.
Berkhart M. Mrs. res. Wayne.
Beyea W. res. State.
Bliss William, res. Court.
Boswell F. res. Church.
Botham Thomas H., res. Church.
Boughton James, res. Church.
Boughton Curtis, res. Court.
Boughton J. res. Wayne.
Bovee E. res. Market.
Boyne John, res. Court.
Brayman A. res. Market.
Brentis John, res. Church.
Brewer J. W. res. State.
Briggs Spencer, res. Court.
Brownell L. A. res. State.
Brooks James, res. Court.
Brown George, res. Main.
Brown R. res. Water.
Brown H. Samuel, cor. Broad and State.
Bryne John, res. Court.
Bruce C. E. res. Hoyt House.
Bruce A. M. res. Hoyt House.
Brown Wm. res. Church.
Burrows T. res. Pleasant.
Bunbery D. E. res. Court.

Caldwell J. C. res. State.
Canavan J. res. State.
Carley G. C. res. State.
Cassiday R. Mrs. res. Port.
Caswell George, res. Main.
Chadwick G. J. res. Main.
Chase Mrs. res. Pleasant.
Chambers John, res. Church.
Chamberlin O. res. Broad.
Chapman Daniel, res. Main.
Chapman Warren, res. Broad.
Chrest C. res. Church.
Chrest M. res. Main.

Church William, res. Church.
Clamfoot B. Mrs. res. Bark.
Clapp G. S. res. cor Broad and State.
Clock A. res. State.
Coleman J. E. res. State.
Collins Frederick, res. Main.
Congdon H. E. res. Court.
Cook Mrs. res. Front.
Crall W. B. res. Wayne.
Crane C. F. Mrs. res. Main.
Crane D. B. Dr. res. State,
Crane E. D. res. State.
Cromer William, res. Court.
Crosby A. res. Church.
Cross Robert, res. Church.
Culp John, res. Main.
Cushman M. H. Mrs. res. Wayne.

Dalke Mrs. res. Court.
Danforth Samuel, res. Main.
DeGerges Joseph, res. Church.
Dempster J. res. Court.
DePuy T. J. res. Main.
Detumble John, res. Court.
Dewitt Charles, res. Main.
Duncan Mrs. res. Court.
Deckersen R. J. Mrs. res. State.
Dunbar Samuel, res. Court.
Dutch A. res. Wayne.
Dutch J. res. Port.

Earl Mrs. res. Pleasant.
Eckhart Louis, res. Main.
Edwards E. M. res. Front.
Elton Alexander, res. Main.
Enos Mrs. (Light House) res. Front.

Fabier G. res. Court.
Fagan P. res. Port.
Farley H. res. Wayne.
Fassett G. W. res. Main.

Ferris Amos, res. Church.
Firch F. Mrs. res. Second Front.
Forbes George, res. State.
Forbes James, res. Front.
Force Louis, res. Main.
Fowler D. S. res. State.
Franz W. res. Wayne.
Freund W. res. Ship, over saloon.
Frick J. res. Wayne.
Frick William, res. State.
Fry John, res. Church.

Garken Jacob, res. Church.
Gallinger R. res. Court.
Garner A. Mrs. res. Market.
Geneit William, res. Court.
Geneit Charles, res. Court.
George William, res. Court.
Georgie E. Rev. res. Market.
Gilbert Frank, res. Court.
Godwald E. res. Court.
Gould A. K. Jr. res. Main.
Guernsey, H. C. res. Market.
Guernsey, H. W. res. Main.
Grabfelder Louis, res. Main.
Gragg R. A. Mrs. res. Broad.
Green J. C. res. Main.
Greening B. res. Church.
Grim H. res. Wayne.

Habel W. res. Port.
Habel August, res. Church.
Hager Joseph, res. Court.
Hager Frank, res. Court.
Hager Joseph, res. Main.
Hamilton, N. A. res. Broad.
Hannon Samuel, res. State.
Harman George, res. Wayne.
Hart William, res. Church.
Hatch J. H. res, State.
Hauser Frederick, res. Church.

Havlin M. res. Water.
Hawley John, res. Main.
Haydin Mrs. res. Church.
Haywood Charles P. res. Main.
Hedrick August, res. Church.
Henning J. res. Water.
Herring August, res. Court.
Heyer Henry, res Church.
Higman John, res. Court.
Higman W. E. res. Main.
Hildebrandt J. Mrs. res. Second Front.
Hill William, res. Main.
Hoffman Herman, res. Main.
Holland Dr. res. Market.
Holt Albert, res. Court.
Hosbien Robert, res. Main.
Howard M. Mrs. res. Market.
Hone J. V. res. Jones.
Howland R. res. Wayne.
Hudson Robert, res. Front.
Hughson J. J. res. Broad.
Hummel A. res. Main.

Irish C. res. Ship.

Jacobs J. res. Price.
Jeffrey J. M. res. Main.
Jenkins D. res. Market.
Jennings George, res. Main.
Jennings Henry, res. Main.
Jordan Francis, res. Main.
Jordan F. C. res. Pleasant.
Jordan John, res. Church.
Jones Alexander, res. State.
Jones Robert, res. Main.

Kawalkee Charles, res. Main.
Kedzie A. S. res. State.
Keller Mrs. res. Court.
Kent Henry, res. Main.
Kepler John, res. Front.

Keyser Vincent, res. Court.
Kibler John, res. Ship, over saloon.
Kilpatrick Frank, res. Court.
Kilpatrick William, res. Ship.
Kinan S. L. res. State.
King B. F. res. State.
King George, res. Port.
King H. F. res. Front.
Kissenger George, res. Minn.
Kissenger L. Mrs. res. Pearl.
Knout Louis, res. State.

Lamond Alexander, res. Court.
Langley H. K. Mrs. res. Main.
Larkin L. res. Front.
Lawler C. M. res. Front.
Leght John, res. Church.
Lessing John, res. Church.
Lessing W. res. Church.
Lessing W. res. Broad.
Livingstone Henry, res. Court.
Livingstone L. Mrs. res. Main.
Loesher Joseph, res. Second Front.
Loesher Paul, res. Church.
Loftis D. res. Wayne.
Long Joseph, res. Ship.
Lorschir A. Mrs. res. Wayne.
Lounge Frank, res. Church.
Lynch N. res. Church.
Lynch J. V. res. Broad.
Lyon W. R. res. Court.

McFall J. M. res. Ship.
McIntire J. res. Ship.
McLinn L. J. res. Main.
Mack Frederick, res. Main.
Mangin M. res. Second Front.
Marsh C. res. State.
Martin John, res. Main.
Mathews Richard, res. Court.
Maynard Leslie, res. Main.

Maynard W. H. res. Main.
Meck John, res. Court.
Melsheimer B. res. Water.
Melsheimer C. res. Church.
Melsheimer Jacob, res. Water.
Merchant L. J. res. Elm.
Meyer Frederick, res. Court.
Miller N. res. Market.
Mills C. res. State.
Millspaugh C. A. res. Second Front.
Minehana D. res. Pearl.
Mitchell Mark, res, Court.
Moat Conrad, res. Main.
Mollhagen Henry, res. Church.
Morelock F. res. Wayne.
Morris W. M. res. Main.
Morrison A. H. res. cor. Broad and State.
Morrison C. res. Market.
Moulton J. N. res. Pleasant.
Moulton Charles, res. Main.
Mulhagen C. res. Wayne.

Newbrandt L. res. State.
Noonan J. res. Port.

O'Hara Thomas, res. Front.
Olds George, res. Front.
Olds Lester, res. Front.
O'Leary Petus, res. Church.
Olson L. res. Pearl.
Ormsbee Mrs. res. Main.
Orthouse L. res. Wayne.
Ott William, res. Church.

Page N. S. res. Second Front.
Palmer E. res. Main.
Palmer E. C. res. State.
Parker R. D., M. D. res. State.
Parks S. H. Dr., res. Pleasant.
Parrick C. res. Port.
Parsons Mrs. res. State.

Patton C. L. Mrs. res. State.
Paul G. W. res. State.
Percival Frank, res. Court.
Perkins A. B. res. Main.
Perkins A. E. res. State.
Perkins E. B. res. State.
Peterson A. res. Church.
Peterson J. res. Wayne.
Peterson John, res. Main.
Phillips T. res. State.
Plumb W. M. res. Court.
Platt G. W. res. State.
Pooler A. res. Front.
Potter A. L. res. State.
Potter C. B. res. Wayne.
Potter Fred, res. Court.
Potter Mrs. res. Court.
Powell John, res. Church.
Powell S. A. res. State.
Preston A. L. Mrs. res. State.
Preston W. A. res. State.

Rahn Frank. res. Church.
Ransom T. T. res. Front.
Ransom W. B. res. State.
Ray H. W. res. State.
Reader P. res. Broad.
Rector O. D. res. Broad.
Reynolds E. res. Wayne.
Ricaby M. res. Pleasant.
Rice G. res. Main.
Rice Nelson, res. Main.
Richards A. D. res. Wayne.
Richie Samuel, res. Court.
Rigney C. res. Church.
Riley G. W. res. Second Front.
Ripley C. res. Port.
Ristoe Peter, res. Church.
Ritenhouse C. res. Court.
Raget W. res. Water.

Robertson J. res. Wayne.
Rockwell H. C. Dr. res. Park.
Rodewalt F. res. Church.
Rowe C. res. Water.
Rowe L. res. Second Front.
Ruler Charles, res. Court.
Russ Charles, res. Court.
Russell C. M. res. Wayne.

Sanger Jacob, res. Court.
Sauerbier Edward, res Main.
Sauerbier Fred., res Main.
Sauerbier William, res Main.
Schembeck M. res. Port.
Schoenbeck August, res. Front.
Scott A. H., M. D. res. State.
Seils B. res. Court.
Shafer John, res. Church.
Shaw J. C. res. State.
Shearer H. res. Wayne.
Shearer T. res. Wayne.
Shepard A. res. State.
Shepard Mont, res. Main.
Shultz Martin, res. Court.
Shyer E. W. Mrs. res. State.
Sibley J. res. State.
Silver H. res. State.
Skinner W. H. H. res. Port.
Slattery John, res. Church.
Simpson Vincent, res. Church.
Slenesker John, res. Main.
Smith George, res. Broad.
Smith Herman, res. Court.
Smith J. Mrs. res. Pearl.
Smith John, res. Court.
Smith P. A. res. Main.
Smith William, res. Pleasant.
Smith William, res. Church.
Snyder E. D. res. Front.
Snyder L. res. Price.

Spaulding K. Mrs. res. Broad.
Sprague W. B., res. State.
Springer Charles. res. Court.
Springsteen B. M. res. State.
Stevens A. E. res. Ship.
Stevens W. H. res. State.
Stevens S. J. res. Ship.
Stebbins L. res. Main.
Stores John, res. Main.
Stines E. G. res. Pleasant.
Stines H. E. res. State.
Stines R. res. Price.
Strain Mrs. res. Court.
Stralow W. res. Park.
Stratton R. F. Dr. res. Broad.
Sweet C. C. res. Front.
Sweet Ogden, res. Front.
Swethman August, res. Court.
Swift F. B. res. Court.

Tanner L. A. res. Front.
Talman George, res. State.
Taylor Frank, res. Front.
Terry N. res. Elm.
Thison Joseph, res. Court.
Thmime W. res. Wayne.
Townsend T. R. res. State.
Truax H. A. res. State.
Tryon M. res. Court.

Vail E. C. B. res. State.
Vance Frank, res. Church.
Vandecker B. res. Church.
Vesey L. L. res. Broad.
Wallace John, res. State.
Walters G. Mrs. res. Church.
Ward H. C. res. State.
Ward W. P. res. State.
Warner F. Mrs. res. Market.
Waters William, res. Church.
Watkins J. res. Wayne.

Watson M. Mrs. res. Wayne.
Weaver John, res. Church.
Weaver William, res. Main.
Webster A. K., M. D. res. State.
Wecklen Peter, res. Main.
Weldon Gilbert, res. Main.
Wells A. res. State.
Wells A. W. res. Front.
Wells J. D. res. Main.
Wescott William, res. Front.
Westfall F. res. Port.
White K. Mrs. res. Pearl.
Wightman W. R. A. res. Court.
Wilcklen H. res. Broad.
Wilkinson John, res. Front.
Williams Mrs. res. Court.
Wilson John, res. Front.
Winchill J. B. res. Park,
Wirtz Fred, res. Court.
Witherel S. res. State.
Wolff Frank, res. Front.
Wolford Joseph, res. Court.
Wood A. S. res. Main.

Yanders Frank, res. Court.
Youngs W., res. Park

Zekind H. M., res. State.
Zaramba Henry, res. Main.

JOSEPH LONG,
SALOON.

On Draught and In Bottles

The Celebrated Ph. Best Brewing Co.'s Beer,

Also Cigars & Choice Liquors.

GIVE ME A CALL.

Ship St., near Hoyt House, St. Joseph, Mich.

ROLLINS PUBLISHING COMPANY'S

Classified Business Directory,

OF

ST. JOSEPH.

American Express Co., M. & A. Shepard, agents, 30 State.
Anderson Carl, machinist, Water.
Baldrey Alfred, agt. C. & M. L. S. R. R., foot of Broad.
Barlow Music Hall, Main nr. Market.
Barnes William Rev., standard religious books, 16 State.
Bate G. A. Mrs., millinery and dressmaking, 36 State.
Bell David, tonsorial artist, ship n. Hoyt House.
Bell Josephine Mrs., hair dresser and hair work manufacturer, Ship nr. State.
Bell Lewis, tonsorial artist and dealer in chignons, wigs, curls, etc., 33 State.
Brewer J. W., justice of the peace, office, City Hall, cor. Main and Broad.
Brown Hiram, custom house officer and justice of the peace, Morrison block No. 1, State.
Brown Richard, cooper, nr. foot State.
Brown, S. H., propr. Park Hotel, cor. Broad and State.
Bruce A. M., propr. Hoyt House, Ship.
Bunbery D. E., saloon, 10 State.
Caldwell James C., livery, sale and feed stable, State s. of Broad.
Canavan J. A. boots and shoes, harness and leather, 33 State.

Carpenter, L. & Co., mfrs. of fruit crates, salesroom 18 State, factory, Benton Harbor.
Central Meat Market, Lewis Eckert, propr., e. s. Main s. of Pleasant.
Chambers C W., dry goods and clothing, 47 State.
Chicago and Michigan Lake Shore Railroad, passenger and freight depots, foot of Broad, C. M. Lawler, ass't. sup't. (See advt).
Chrest William, grocer, restaurant, cigars, etc., Ship.
Church Louis J., mfr. shot guns, rifles, etc., cor. State and Ship.
City Hall, cor. Main and Broad.
Clapp George S., attorney at law, n. e. cor. State and Pleasant, over First National Bank.
Clapp Jennie M. Miss, fancy goods, 32 State.
Clapp & Fyfe, attorneys at law, cor. State and Pleasant, over First National Bank.
Clarke James R., deputy sheriff and insurance agent, State, over First National Bank.
Clock L. D. & Bro., watchmakers and jewelers, 43 State.
Colburn & Gregg, millinery, 32 State.
Cooper Ice Co., Henry Cooper, manager.
Crane E. D., druggist, bookseller and stationer, 29 State.
Crosby & Hart, barbers and dealers in hair goods and cigars, 21 State.
Custom House Office, Hiram Brown, officer, Morrison block No. 1, State.
Domestic Sewing Machine, M. & A. Shepard, agents, 30 State.
Donaldson Walter, saddle and harness manufacturer and insurance agent, 35 State.
DePuy Theo. J., attorney at law, over 48 State cor Pleasant.
Dudley, Jennings & Co., publishers Lake Shore Daily News, n. e. cor. State and Pleasant.
Eckert Lewis, propr. Central Meat Market, e. s. Main s. of Pleasant.
First National Bank, n. e. cor. State and Pleasant, organized Sept. 1871. Capital $50,000. W. E. Higman, prest., James Baley cashier, O. O. Jordon, ass't. cashier.
Forbes James, groceries, crockery, glass and lampware, flour and feed, 45 State.
Forbes James, groceries, flour, feed, crockey, etc., 45 State.

Freund William, saloon, Ship, bet. State and Main.
Fyfe Law C., attorney at law, cor. State and Pleasant, over First National Bank.
Glass W. D., night telegraph operator C. & M. L. S. R. R., foot of Broad.
Gilbert Frank, mfr and dealer in boots and shoes, 7 State.
Goodrich Transportation Line, A. H. Morrison, agent, Morrison Dock, foot of Water.
Gottwald Edward, blacksmith, Ship nr. Main.
Grebfelder Lewis, meat market, Main.
Guernsey House, G. Hubbard, prop., State.
Hager J. S., blacksmith, e. s. Main bet. Ship and Pleasant.
Hamilton H. A., attorney at law, over First National Bank.
Hannon Samuel, blacksmithing, carriage and wagon mfr. n. e. cor. State and Elm.
Hauser & McMullen, wagons, carriages, buggies and blacksmithing, 2 and 4 State.
Hendricks August, meat market, Ship bet. State and Main.
Henning John F., bakery, confectionery and lunch room, Ship nr. Main.
Herman George, meat market, Ship bet. State and Main.
Hertges Anthony, tailor, Ship bet. State and Main.
Hevlin Michael, saloon, cor. State and Water.
Hoos Andrew, boarding house and saloon, nr. cor. Ship and Main
Hosbien Robert, furniture, cor. Ship and Main.
Hoyt House, A. M. Bruce, propr., Ship.
Hubbard G., propr. Guernsey House, State.
Hulsart C. C., manager Tivoli, opposite Postoffice.
Kamerer Conrad, Propr. National Hotel cor. Main and Post.
Kent & Bovee, marble works, s. e. cor. Ship and Main.
Keppler John, groceries and meat market.
Kibler John, saloon, Ship bet. State and Main.
King B. F., postmaster, 13 State.
Kuman S. L., ass't agt. C. & M. L. S. R. R., foot and Broad.
Koerber G., groceries, crockery, glassware, tobacco and cigars, Port bet. State and Main.
Kolman Louis, stationery and news depot, Postoffice, 13 State.
Lake Shore Daily News, Dudley, Jennings & Co., publishers, n. e. cor. State and Pleasant.

CHICAGO
AND
MICHIGAN
Lake Shore Railroad.

General Offices:

MUSKEGON, MICHIGAN.

OFFICERS:

NATT. THAYER, Boston, President.

N. THAYER, JR., Boston, Vice President and General Manager, St. Joseph, Mich.

GEO. C. KIMBALL, General Manager and Superintendent.

C. M. LAWLER, Assistant Superintendent, St. Joseph, Mich.

A. M. NICHOLS, General Freight and Passenger Agent, at Grand Rapids, Mich.

HUGH PARK, Auditor.

H. L. BROWN, Assistant General Freight Agent, Muskegon, Mich.

B. BUNN, Cashier and Paymaster, Muskegon, Mich.

R. BOOTH, Master Mechanic, Muskegon, Mich.

R. HUNT & BRESEE, Superintendent of Bridges, St. Joseph, Mich.

A. H. MORRISON,

STORAGE AND

Forwarding Merchant,

MORRISON'S DOCKS,

ST. JOSEPH, - MICH.

AGENT FOR

Goodrich Transportation Company.

Steamers for Chicago Daily at 9 p. m.

Except Saturdays during season of Navigation, and at Chicago connect with Steamers for all ports on Lake Michigan.

General Fire Insurance Agent.

Representing more Insurance Capital than any other office in the United States.

Office, Morrison Block, No. 1 State St.

Langley S. E., livery, sale and feed stable, Main
Lawler C. M., ass't sup't C. & M. L. S. R. R., office foot Broad.
Lee & Wells, prop'rs St. Joseph flouring mills, Water bet. State and Main.
Long Joseph, saloon, Ship bet. State and Front. (See advt.)
Lynch J. V., dry goods and clothing, 28 State.
Lyon W. R., attorney at law, over 32 State.
Marks S. H., physician and surgeon, Pleasant bet. Court and Church.
Marsh Charles, cabinet maker, s. w. cor. State and Pleasant.
Martin John, dry goods, etc., s. s. Ship e. State.
Maynard W. S. & Co., mf'rs of carriages, wagons, sleighs, cutters, etc., cor. Main and Market.
Melsheimer B., saloon, 11 State.
Melsheimer J., saloon and boarding house Water bet. State and Main.
Merchant L. J., editor and proprietor St. Joseph Traveler-Herald, Hoyt Block, cor. Ship and Main.
Morlock F. & Co., saloon, n. w. cor. Ship and Main.
Morrison A. H., storage and forwarding merchant; agent for Goodrich Tranportation Co., and General Fire Insurance agent; senior member of firm of Morrison & Pulasky, offices Morrison Block No. 1, State and foot of Water, Morrison Dock. (See Advt.)
Morrison & Pulasky, mfrs pails, tubs and other woodenware, office Morrison Block No. 1, 42 State (up stairs.)
Moulton Chas. H., stoves, tinware, copper and sheet iron ware, 42 State.
Moulton Mrs. M. K., fancy dry goods and millinery, 43 State.
McLin L. J., Homœopathist, north of Congregationalist church.
National Hotel, Conrad Kamerer, propr, cor. Main and Port.
Olds G. W., cooper, foot State.
Orthouse Lewis, cigar mfrs and dealers in tobacco and cigars, s. s. Ship bet. Front and State.
Palmer E. C., druggist and grocer, 44 and 46 State.
Park Hotel, S. H. Brown, prop'r, cor. State and Broad. (See advt.)
Paul G. W., warehouseman, C. & M. L. S. R. R., foot of Broad.
Perkins House, Geo. Sherman, propr. Ship bet. State and Front.

Pew Bertine, picture frames and upholstering, 16 State.
Platt & Bro., hardware, 14 State.
Postoffice, B. F., King, postmaster, 13 State.
Potter A. L., real estate, insurance and loans, State s. 1st Nat'l Bank, res. State.
Potter & Potter, attorneys, Potter Block, Ship e. of State.
Preston F. J. bakery etc., Preston's Block, n. s. Ship.
Preston W. A., sash, doors, blinds, mouldings, etc., dealer in lumber, lath, shingles. Office and factory foot of Wayne nr. the bridge.
Rahn F. bootmaker, cor. Ship and State.
Ransom T. T., grocer, 26 State cor. Ship.
Ray H. H. & H. W., resident dentists, s. e. cor. State and Ship.
Ricaby Wm., watches, jewelry, books, stationery, music, musical instruments, fancy goods, etc., 48 State cor. Ship.
Ricaby Wm. & Son, publishers St. Joseph Republican, (weekly) over 44 State.
Ricaby's Photograph Gallery, over 46 State.
Rice Z. & Son, general store, groceries, crockery, glassware and lamp goods, 40 State.
Rockwell H. C., dentist, n. w. cor. State and Pleasant.
Ruggles & Ewalt, mfrs of confectionery and dealers in fruits etc., 34 State.
Sauerbier Frederick, groceries, provisions, etc., e. s. Main s. Pleasant.
Scott A. H., physician and surgeon, office 27 State, (up stairs.)
Sesser W. F., photographer, Morrison's block, Ship.
Shepard M. & A., watches, clocks, jewelry, books, stationery, music, musical instruments, etc., agents American Express Co. and Domestic Sewing Machine, 30 State.
Sherman George, prop'r Perkins House, Ship bet. State and Front.
Sibley J., drugs and medicines, cor. State and Ship.
Smith Geo. E., groceries, provisions, flour and feed, etc., 17 and 19 State.
Sordel Albert, shoemaker, Ship bet. State and Main.
Springsteen B. M., physician, 11 State (up stairs.)
St. Joseph Flouring Mills, Lee and Wells, proprs.
St. Joseph Traveler-Herald, (weekly) L. J. Merchant, publisher, Hoyt Block, cor. Ship and Main.

St. Joseph Republican, (weekly) Wm. Ricaby & Son, publishers, over 44 State.
Stebbins Luther, confectioneries, fruit, etc., e. s. Main, 2 doors n. Pleasant.
Stevens Wm. L., propr Tivoli, opposite Postoffice.
Stratton R. F., physician, Broad, opposite Park Hotel.
Sweet C. C. & Bro., general store, cor. State and Ship.
Tanner L. A., carriage trimmer and upholsterer, under 1st National Bank.
Tatman G. B. & Co., meat market, flour, feed and provisions, n. w. cor. State and Ship.
Taylor Francis, merchant tailor and clothier, gents' furnishing goods, hats, caps, etc., 27 State.
The Industrial Spinning and Knitting Works, A. W. Hart, manager.
Tivoli saloon, opposite postoffice.
Townsend F. R. foreman, Traveler-Herald, cor Ship and Main.
Wallace & Barnes, lumber, lath, shingles, fencing, building material, etc., lime, cement and land plaster, foot of State.
Watson John A., law student, Clapp & Fyfe, cor. State and Pleasant.
Webster A. K., physician and surgeon, over 48 State cor. Pleasant.
Weckler Peter, furniture, s. s. Ship, e. State.
Wells A. W. & Co., manufacturers of fruit packages, office and salesroom 9 State.
Western Union Telegraph Co., Sam'l H. Brown, manager, Park Hotel.
Wilcox W. R. & Co., manufacturers of fruit packages, salesroom 6 State, factory w. of the depot. (See advt.)
Wilkinson John, restaurant, etc., 31 State.
Wilson John W., fish market, Water bet. State and Main.
Wolf Frank, saloon, n. e. ship nr. State.
Yore John, groceries and provisions, n. s. Ship and State.
Zekind H. M., dry goods, etc., 38 State.

County Officers of Berrien County.

The Second Judicial District is composed of Berrien and Cass counties; Hon. H. H. Coolidge, Circuit Judge, post office, Niles; regular terms of court commence as follows: Berrien County—On Tuesday next after first day of January, and fourth Tuesdays of March and June, and second Tuesday of October. Cass County—First Tuesdays of March and June, the third Tuesday of September, and the first Tuesday of December.

State Senator, 13th Dist.—Wm. Chamberlain, Three Oaks.
Representatives in State Legislature: 1st Dist.—Silas Ireland, Summerville. 2d Dist.—N. A. Hamilton, St. Joseph. 3d Dist.—Geo. F. Edwards, Niles.

Judge of Probate—Alexander B. Leeds, Berrien Springs.
Sheriff—Richard A. DeMont, Berrien Springs.
County Clerk—E. D. Cooke, Berrien Springs.
Register of Deeds—Wm. H. Marston, Berrien Springs.
County Treasurer—John Tate, Berrien Springs.
Prosecuting Attorney—J. J. Van Riper, Buchanan.
Circuit Court Commissioners—Jas. A. Kellogg, Niles; Law. C, Fyfe, St. Joseph.
Surveyor—John M. Glavin, New Buffalo.
Coroners—Rufus K. Charles, Niles; Jas. Pointer, Benton Harbor.
Fish Inspector—Chas. Mollhagen, St. Joseph.

Board of Supervisors.

The following is the Board-elect for 1878-9:
Buchanan—L. P. Fox, Greenback-Rep.
Berrien—D. H. Ullery, Rep.
Bertrand—J. H. Young, Dem.
Benton—S. L. Van Camp, Rep.
Bainbridge—Chas. C. Kent, Dem.
Chikaming—A. L. Drew, Ind.
Galien—B. R. Stearns, Rep.
Hagar—Dewitt Guy, Dem.
Lake—M. B. Houser, Rep.
Lincoln—A. D. Brown, Rep.
Niles—Wm. B. Davis, Dem.
Niles City—W. A. Reddick, Rep.
Niles City—Frank Brownell, Dem.
New Buffalo—Fred. Gerdes, Dem.
Oronoko—Z. Fisher, Dem.
Pipestone—M. Davis, Dem.
Royalton—A. H. Carlton, Dem.
St. Joseph—E. M. Edwards, Rep.
Sodus—O. Inglesbee, Rep.
Three Oaks—Wm. H. Brocee, Dem.
Watervliet—S. P. Merrifield, Rep.
Weesaw—Geo. Pierce, Rep.

1719284

THE "AUDUBON"
Folding Canvas Canoe,

IS, WITHOUT DOUBT,

THE BEST BOAT

For the purpose intended ever offered.

BEING MADE OF

STRONG CANVAS

Treated so as to make it

*WATER PROOF, DURABLE,
LIGHT, EASILY FOLDED
and TRANSPORTABLE.*

It can be folded and unfolded without the use of any tools, simply with the hands.

We offer the "Audubon" with the confidence which results from years of experimenting and practical knowledge, and with the assurance that it needs only to be tried to give satisfaction.

For prices, discount to dealers, and any further information, address

W. W. BARCUS & CO.

Sole Manufacturers of the

"AUDUBON"

Jobber of Cordage, Twines, &c.

282 S. Water Street,

CHICAGO.

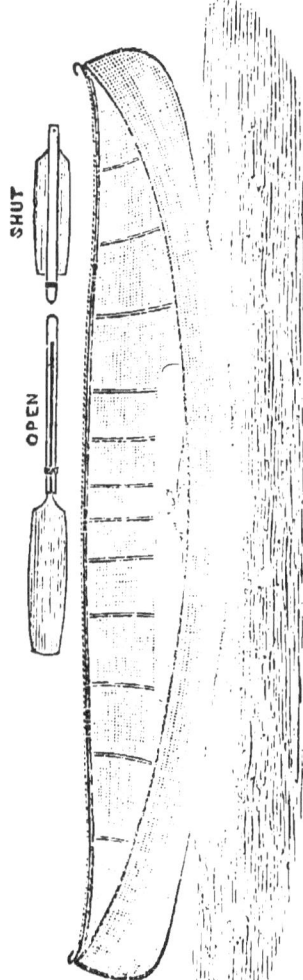

BOAT FOLDED.

W. R. Wilcox & Co.

MANUFACTURERS OF

Fruit Packages

ST. JOSEPH, MICH.

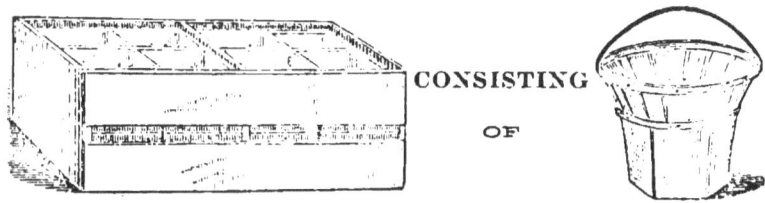

CONSISTING OF

Berry, Grape and Vegetable Boxes, Peach and Grape Baskets, also Clothes Pin Boxes, and all Boxes made out of Veneering.

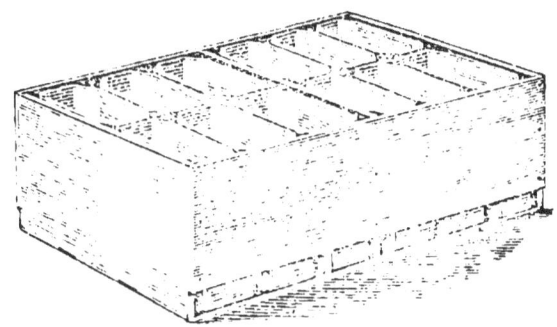

We cannot be UNDERSOLD, and what is more, WE GUARANTEE EVERY PACKAGE we make. COME or SEND to US and buy the BEST the market affords.

Send for Illustrated Price List. All Orders filled Promptly on Short Notice. Goods Packed and delivered at the Depot or Dock free of Charge.

W. R. WILCOX & CO.

Fashionable! Comfortable! Durable!

A combination of these qualities with that of cheapness, in the manufacture of my Boots and Shoes, are the strongest recommendations that I can bring in asking for a continuance of that patronage which has been so long accorded to me by the Chicago public. As heretofore, I shall continue to furnish Boots and Shoes in the very latest styles and of the very best materials, guaranteeing in all cases a PERFECT FIT.

To meet the exigencies of the times, I will make to order in the latest style at the following

LOW PRICES

French Calf Hand Sewed Boots	$10 00	English Grain Leather, English Waukenfast	10 00
American Calf Hand Sewed Boots	9 00	French Calf, Alexia Buckle	8 50
French Calf, Morocco legs Boots	12 00	American Calf, Alexis Buckle	7 50
American Calf, Morocco legs	11 00	French Calf, Alexis Tie	8 00
Patent Leather, Morocco legs	14 00	American Calf, Alexis Tie	7 00
Alligator feet, Morocco legs	15 00	French Calf Creole Gaiters	8 50
Grained Leather Napoleon Boots	15 00	American Calf Creole Gaiters	7 50
French Kip Napoleon Boots	16 00	Congress Gaiters, French Calf	8 00
English Grain Napoleon Boots	17 00	Congress Gaiters, American Calf	7 00
Congress Shoes, French Calf	7 50	Front Lace Shoes, French Calf	8 00
Congress Shoes, American Calf	7 00	Front Lace Shoes, American Calf	7 00
Congress Shoes, all one piece French Calf	8 00	Button Gaiters, French Calf	9 00
Congress Shoes, all one piece, American Calf	7 50	Button Gaiters, American Calf	8 00
Oxford Tie, French Calf	7 00		
Oxford Tie, American Calf	6 50	**EXTRAS.**	
Oxford Tie, whole vamps, French Calf	8 00	Tips	50
Oxford Tie, whole vamps, American Calf	7 50	Wrinkles	50
Webster Tie, French Calf	7 50	Box Toes	50
Webster Tie, American Calf	7 00	Patent Leather	1 00
Webster Tie, Patent Leather back	8 00	Cloth Tops	50
French Calf Protection Gaiters	9 00	Hand-worked Button Holes	50
American Calf Protection Gaiter	8 00	Whole Vamps	50
French Calf English Waukenfast	9 00	Imitation Button	50
American Calf English Waukenfast	8 00	Double Soles	50
		Tap Soles	1 00

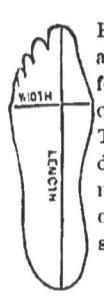

Persons out of the city can order Boots and Shoes by following my directions for Self-Measurement. Place the foot on paper, and trace outline as Fig. 1. Then use an ordinary tape-measure draw so there is no slack and give exact measurement in inches, and fractions of each part of the foot as Fig. 2, and send to.

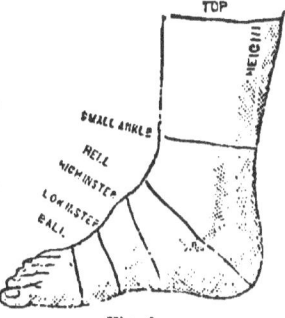

Fig. 1. Fig. 2.

J. B. MACKEL,

The French Boot-Maker,

61 S. Clark St.   Opposite Sherman House,   **Chicago.**

St. Joseph Republican,

A

WEEKLY DEMOCRATIC PAPER.

WM. RICABY & SON, Publishers.

Is published at 44 State street, St. Joseph, Michigan, every Wednesday. Subscription $1.50 per year. It is the only Democratic paper in the place; is well patronized, and consequently is a desirable

ADVERTISING MEDIUM,

AS WELL AS AN ORIGINAL HOME, LOCAL AND EDITORIAL SHEET.

JOB WORK,

THE REPUBLICAN has every facility for doing job work, plain or ornamental, and does it at reasonable rates.

TRAVELER - HERALD.

Published every Saturday Morning

——)BY(———

LEONARD J. MERCHANT.

ST. JOSEPH, MICHIGAN.

TERMS: $1.50 a year, if paid in advance; if not paid in advance, $2.00 will be charged. These terms will be strictly adhered to.

PUBLISHING COMPANY'S

Benton Harbor

AND

ST. JOSEPH

DIRECTORY,

Containing Historical and Descriptive Sketches of both
places, and a full list of the Residents, together
with a Business Directory, and a
full record of Fruit
Growers and
Shippers.

CHICAGO:
ROLLINS PUBLISHING COMPANY,
161 LASALLE STREET,
1878.

BENTON HARBOR.

HISTORICAL.

Soon after Michigan emerged from its territorial minority and was admitted to the Union as a full fledged state, the township of Benton Harbor was organized, in 1837. Prior to that time St. Joseph township included Benton, Bainbridge, Watervleit and Hager. The earliest election in the new township was held at the village of Millburg which had been laid out in 1835, by Jehiel Enos and Amos S. Anderson. The former of these was one of Benton's earliest settlers. Population grew slowly for a number of years, Eleazer Morton had emigrated from the East to Kalamazoo in 1834, whence he moved to St. Joseph in the following year and settled on the farm now occupied by Henry C. Morton. At that time the place on the bluff where Charles Hall resides was occupied by L. L. Johnson and a Mr. Dalton lived on the Kline place.

The locality was not regarded by early settlers as favorable for cultivation, the sandy soil appearing sterile to their eyes. In 1845 the entire population of the township was but 237. The only suggestion of future greatness for the place and not an apparent one at the time, lay in the peach orchard owned by Mr. Morton, who made the earliest shipment of peaches from the neighborhood in 1841. By and by it began to be noticed that fruit orchards near the lake escaped the destruction that came to those inland, by means of cold weather, and the attention of fruit growers was attracted to the vicinity. The profits being realized by the few already on the spot, added to the market advantages offered by propinquity to Chicago and other large places, stimulated

this favorable consideration. Among the first to engage largely in the peach culture here was George Parmerlee, who in 1848 started a small orchard of two acres. This area he increased from year to year until it reached ninety acres, and a few years ago sold the whole for $43,000. In 1857 the Cincinnati orchard, the largest in the State of Michigan was set out. In 1859 Sterne Brunson bought eighty acres of land the boundaries of which included part of the present village of Benton Harbor. He had visited St. Joseph thirty years before with the idea of buying land and engaging in fruit culture, but Major Britain had given him discouraging statements as to the nature of the climate, soil, etc., and so the project was abandoned for the time and he bought a farm at Elkhart upon which he resided until 1859 as stated.

Since the year last mentioned great changes have taken place in the appearance of the county. At that time, where now the residences of thriving citisens abound, and where fine avenues lead the visitor past long reaches of country covered with rich orchards, the land was covered with a primeval forest. The wealth-compelling peach tree had not come into the locality as yet, to rout the aboriginal oak and beech. In 1860 a village was laid out on the flat near the marsh, by Sterne Brunson, B. C. Lewis, and others, and the place was known for some time as Brunson's Harbor. Gates & Bell bought the first village lot for $60 on six year's time, and the second, the one next east of the above, was disposed of for $50 on five year's time. The early settlers had thought of a village on that side of the marsh, with a canal to connect it with the river, but the idea never took any practical form until the energetic mind of Mr. Brunson was devoted to the project. The success of the scheme has won that gentleman great honor among the people of the section and he is regarded as one of the best and most valuable friends Benton Harbor ever possessed.

A committee was appointed by the citisens of Benton Harbor, to obtain subscriptions for the canal, consisting of Sterne Brunson, Henry C. Morton and Charles C. Hull. By far the heaviest part of the load, however, fell upon the shoulders of the committee itself, the members of which also superintended the construction. Martin Green, of Chicago took the contract for digging a canal twenty-five feet wide and eight feet deep, and the same was finished in 1862. The schooner J. C. Shank was the first boat to

enter it and come up to the village. In the latter part of 1861, the business houses of the village consisted of the following establishments: Charles J. Smith, groceries and dry goods; H. L. Harris, groceries; M. G. Lampert, watches and jewelry; and Hatch & Durry—the latter where Robbin's place of business is at present.

The name was changed to Benton Harbor in 1865, and since that time the advancement of the place has been rapid in manufactures, commerce, and the value of property. The canal has been widened to fifty feet, numbers of fine business structures have been erected, elegant residences abound and large warehouses suggest the commercial importance of the town. The corporate limits are rapidly extending, and ground that could have been bought a few years ago for fifty dollars an acre is now worth at least one thousand dollars. The first house of worship in Benton Harbor—the Congregational—was built in 1868 and some time afterward the Methodist and Baptist denominations erected substantial and handsome edifices. A large union school house, complete in every appointment was secured to the village at a cost of $30,000. By the expenditure of $16,000 the community has acquired railroad facilities, likely to be increased by the building of the projected Elkhart and Lake Michigan Railroad. Three excellent newspapers furnish the little world of Benton Harbor with knowledge of all that transpires in the greater world; these are the *Times*, *Palladium* and the *Lake Shore Daily News*. The first number of the *Palladium* was issued October 9, 1868 by L. J. Merchant, who afterward disposed of the property to J. P. Thresher; subsequently it came into the possession of the present owner Charles E. Reeves. The *Lake Shore Daily News* is published simultaneously every evening in St. Joseph and Benton Harbor. This first venture of the locality in daily journalism was inaugurated last year by Dudley, Jennings & Co., and bids fair to become a most successful enterprise. Established in the face of four weekly papers, it has already made itself a household favorite and necessity. Coming before the people at tea time, it and its spicy items are the subject of conversation. Its happy way of giving all the important news, home and foreign, in a condensed shape, enables the busy people of this section to keep posted on the events of the day without poring over column after column of dispatches as in the city dailies. It has thus already become the favorite adver-

tising medium of this section. The population of the village is about 1,300; and 2,600 is approximately the number of inhabitants in the township of Benton. The leading pursuits of the people here are related to fruit culture, about half of the entire product of the region finding its outlet by way of Benton Harbor.

LEADING PEOPLE AND ENTERPRISES.

Having referred in general to the prosperity of Benton Harbor and to the influences that have created that prosperity, it is not out of place to speak personally of some of the citisens and of their enterprises. Perhaps a good many may not be remembered, but if so it is because their names do not occur to the publisher, at the moment.

Among the most prominent concerns of the village that of Higman Heath & Co. is distinguished. Mr. Higman is president of the First National Bank. Mr. Heath is a wealthy fruit grower and Mr. Bailey, cashier of the bank and manager is the "Co."

Among the first of Benton Harbor's distinguished citizens, the Hon. Henry C. Morton is honored for the energy he has displayed in furthering the interests of his town and section. He was born at Alexander, Genesee county, New York, January 27, 1817, where he lived until 1834, in which year his family moved to Kalamazoo. In 1835 he settled at Benton Harbor, and in the year following bought 400 acres on the east side of the river, upon which he still resides, the original tract forming part of the present property. Mr. Morton commenced to raise fruit—peaches and apples—in 1840, and set out the third orchard started in the neighborhood. He was elected to the State Legislature in 1862, and served one term, declining a re-election which was unanimously tendered him by his constituents. He cast his first presidential vote for General Harrison, and continued a strict and consistent Whig until the formation of the Republican party, the fortunes of which he has followed unswervingly to the present day. In 1864 he was appointed Postmaster, and continued in that office until removed by President Johnson; but Mr. Morton declined to surrender the office, and held on until reappointed by General Grant. After that he occupied the office until 1873, when he resigned in favor of J. P. Thresher. Throughout a long career of usefulness, the Hon. Henry C. Morton has enjoyed the confidence and respect of all

State as well as in Benton Harbor, is the extensively known _____ factory of Messrs. Ingham, Leslie & Co. They manufacture, and deal in fruit packages of all kinds, veneers, crimped elm headlinings, cheese box hoops, cigar box veneers, and many other similar articles. Messrs. Ingham, Leslie & Co., have acquired a wide reputation for the goods of their manufacture, which they ship in large quantities to all parts of the country. The members of the firm are leading citisens of the locality and of the commonwealth; and are justly regarded as entitled to the respect and esteem of the community, which, indeed they enjoy completely.

One of the commercial enterprises of general value recently introduced to Benton Harbor, is the manufacture and sale of Wentworth's Centennial Bed Spring, patented August 29th, 1876. The proprietors of this useful and valuable invention, Messrs. Wentworth Bros. conduct factories both at Benton Harbor, and at Decatur, Illinois, from which points they have introduced the Centennial Bed, generally throughout the country. The business, at present large enough to employ the full capacity of the two factories, is growing to such dimensions, that factories in other localities will probably have to be established before long. At the Benton Harbor house, Wentworth Bros. sell their manufacture at wholesale and retail, and dispose of state and county rights on the most reasonable terms.

The navy of Benton Harbor is elsewhere referred to in the paragraph devoted to the steamer Messenger. As the lake traffic is of the greatest importance to the vicinity, so the leading people engaged in navigation, commercially or professionally are regarded as distinguished citisens. Prominent among the latter, mention should be made of Captain A. C. Bartlett, the brave and courteous commander of the "Messenger," of Graham, Morton & Co.'s line.

The traveling community as a rule judge of cities and towns to a great extent by the character of their hotels, and not without reason, for where there are not any good public houses, it is pretty conclusive evidence that business is poor and enterprise lacking. In respect of hotels, Benton Harbor is fortunate, as its commerce and industries justify it in supporting three very handsomely, two of which take unchallenged rank as first-class houses.

The American House kept by Alonzo Vincent, is located in the business centre of the town, near the post-office, express-office, and bank, and is everything that could be desired in the way of accommodation for permanent or transient guests. The house is neatly and tastefully furnished, the table excellent, and the host and his assistants polite and attentive.

The Gartley House, Fonger & Stewart, proprietors, is deservedly one of the most popular hotels in Western Michigan. It is new and furnished completely throughout with every thing that modern ingenuity has devised to render hotel life comfortable and attractive. The Gartley House is on Water street, conveniently near the post-office, steamboat docks and depot. The extent and class of patronage enjoyed by this house, is the only encomium it needs as to the character of entertainment offered to the public by Messrs. Fonger & Stewart.

Another very excellent hotel the Colfax House, is kept by S. L. Vincent, and is well patronised by citisens and visitors.

Colby & Co., manufacturers of fruit packages, conduct an extensive manufacturing business, supplying all the neighboring and many distant markets with their popular, useful and durable wares. They make specialties of the "Benton Gift Egg Case," and grape and peach baskets with patent railroad top.

L. Carpenter & Co. are proprietors of the Benton Harbor and St. Joseph fruit package factories where an entire line of goods of that character are made and sold wholesale and retail. They also manufacture tea caddies and all other boxes made of veneering. Parties desirous of procuring any goods of the above description should send to the firm for their illustrated price list.

H. W. Williams, whose office and saw mill is on the territorial road between Benton Harbor and St. Joseph, has one of the finest saw mills in the country and does an extensive lumber business; his connections reaching all over Michigan and the West generally. Mr. Williams manufactures and vends wholesale and retail, all kinds of hard and soft lumber. He makes a specialty of filling bills for ordered lumber and also manufactures all kinds of pickets.

Another large manufacturing and commercial lumber house is J. H. Graham. & Co., near the depot. Mr. Crawford the junior member of the firm makes his headquarters in Chicago, in which market a large amount of their product is disposed of.

Eldridge & Robbins deal heavily in all kinds of lumber and are as well the principal firm of contractors and builders in Benton Harbor. The firm consists of B. B. Eldridge and W. P. Robbins, the latter a popular and much patronized notary public and conveyancer for Berrien county.

One of the principal commercial advantages enjoyed by Benton Harbor, is the ample and fast connection maintained with Chicago and the West by the steamer line of Graham, Morton & Co. The splendid freight and passenger steamer Messenger of this line runs regularly, leaving the company's dock at the foot of Wabash avenue every morning at 10 o'clock, Saturdays and Sundays excepted; on Saturdays it leaves at 11:30 P. M. Returning, the steamer leaves Benton Harbor every evening at 9 o'clock, Saturdays excepted. The trip, occupying five hours either way, is the pleasantest across the lake. As an extra inducement to travel, the line has recently reduced its fare to the low rate of $2, berth included, for the round trip; or $1.50 each way. Freights are carried as low as by any other line. The company also take freight for Hager, Riverside, Colona, Watervliet, Hartford, Bangor, Breedsville, Grand Junction, Millburgh, Pipestone, Eau Claire, Berrien Centre, and Shanghai. Messrs. Graham, Morton & Co. also do a general dockage and storage business at reasonable rates. The

following first-class propellers run from their docks: The R. C. Brittain, for Saugatuck; the Douglas Trader, for Pentwater; and the Snook, for Whitehall and Montague.

Mr. L. McClane has a large and finely cultivated nursery situated one mile southeast of the village, which enjoys a reputation far and wide for the excellence of all its productions. Nothing that art or capital could accomplish has been spared to make this nursery the equal of any in the West.

The firm of Pitcher, Jones & Sonner conduct the largest establishment in Benton Harbor in the line of business followed by them. They deal very extensively in dry goods, carpets, clothing, gentlemen's furnishing goods, hats, caps, ladies shoes, oilcloths, etc. The warerooms of the house are on Main street.

As it is not considered consistent with the canons of professional etiquette to write anything concerning doctors and lawyers which might have the appearance of advertising them, it is only competent to remark that Benton Harbor has several resident members of of the learned professions, distinguished in their several callings. At the bar A. B. Riford, Esq. and A. Plummer, Esq., stand high, and are justly trusted with a large business together with the confidence of their fellow citisens. In the healing art Doctor John Bell occupies a well earned pre-eminence.

Of the younger men of Benton Harbor, there are many who well deserve mention in connection with the manufacturing and business interests of the town. Unfortunately there is not space enough within the limits of this sketch to treat of them fully; a couple of samples will have to answer. Mr. H. S. Morton, son of the Hon. H. C. Morton, is the popular clerk of the steamer Messenger, and about as well and favorably known, both at home and in Chicago, as a young and rising business man could desire. Mr. Thomas A. Walker, connected with the same line, and in their office at Benton Harbor, is everybody's friend in the town. He has lived here fifteen years, and has been with Graham, Morton & Co. about four years. His abilities and genial manner have made him hosts of valuable friends, and his rise to business prominence may be certainly predicted.

Township Officers.

S. L. Vancamp, Supervisor.
Geo. M. Valentine, Clerk.
Andrew J. Kidd, Treasurer.
A. Plummer, Justice of the Peace.
Benj. F. Rounds, Comm'r Highways.
John C. Lawrence, Sup't Schools.
Henry A. Radkliffe, School Inspector.
James F. Higbee, Drain Commissioner.
Cashan Burr, Constable.
Geo. A. Slater, "
Lewis H. Swisher "
Martin J. Hill, "

Board of Trustees.

Village of Benton Harbor, John W. Leslie, President. Rod man M. Worden, B. B. Eldridge, John Allmandinger, Judson Russell, H. W. Williams, J. N. Burridge; P. M. Kenney, Treasurer; Henry L. Pitcher. Clerk; Jos. W. Weiman, Assessor; Cashan Burr, Marshal.

Churches.

CONGREGATIONAL CHURCH.—J. C. Thompson, Pastor.
BAPTIST CHURCH.—Rev. J. D. Pulis, Pastor.
METHODIST EPISCOPAL CHURCH.—Robbins' Hall, Rev. J. K. Stark, Pastor.

Societies.

YOUNG MEN'S CHRISTIAN ASSOCIATION.—Robbins' Hall, Friday night. H. W. Miller, President. Warren Lamport, Secretary.

LAKE SHORE LODGE, No. 298, A. F. and A. M.—Reynold's block, Monday evening. John Bell, W. M. F. Morley, Secretary.

BENTON HARBOR GRANGE, No. 122.—First and third Saturdays of each month. Hall over L. L. Clark's grocery. E. Nickerson, W. M. W. J. Nott, Secretary.

I. O. G. T.—Benton Harbor Lodge No. 844. Wednesday evening. Hall over L. L. Clark's grocery. Hatie Reed, Sec. I. R. Dunning, W. C. T.

I. O. O. F.—Benton Lodge No. 132. Tuesday evening. Hall over Brunson & Johnson's hardware store. T. A. Walker, Sec. C. A. Warner, N. G.

ROLLINS PUBLISHING COMPANY'S

Benton Harbor City Directory

FOR 1878-79.

Adams, E. C, res Main.
Adams, Geo., res. cor. Boughton and Centre.
Adams, J, res. Main.
Allison, D. S., res. cor. Territorial and 6th.
Allkins, Henry, res. Cherry.
Allmandinger, Andrew, res. cor. Lake & Center.
Almendinger, Jno. M., res. Territorial.
Antisdale, H., res. cor. Maple and Pipestone.
Antisdale, Silas, res. Michigan.
Austin, S. M., res. Pipestone.

Babcock, Chas., res. Maple.
Babcock, Geo., res. Cherry.
Bailey, James, res. Belleview.
Barrow, Mrs., res. Territorial.
Banske, Albert, res. Elm.
Baute, Henry, res. Water.
Baute, John, res. N. Water.
Bell, John, res. cor. Belleview and Michigan.
Bell, John, M. D., Main.

Bell, Joseph, res. cor. Elm and 6th.
Belton, Joseph, res. cor. Brunson av. & Church.
Benedict, H. C., res. Territorial.
Bird, —., res. Broadway.
Boswell, Wm., res. cor. Oak and Michigan.
Bower, John, res. Territorial.
Boyle, C. S., res. Territorial.
Boyle, Stephen, res. cor. Territorial and 4th.
Boyne, —., res. Elm.
Bradley, Wm. E., res. Town Line.
Bramwell, Ed., res. Pipestone.
Breithanpt, J. M., res. Maple.
Brooks, Perry, res. cor. Oak and Michigan.
Brown, M. Mrs., res. Lake.
Brown, Wells, res. Michigan.
Brunson, Allen, res. Pipestone.
Brunson, Rufus, res. Pipestone.
Brunson, Rush, res. Washington.
Bryant, G. H., res. Pipestone.
Bryant, W. C., res. Centre.
Buchanan, Mary Mrs., res. Centre.
Burr, Cush., res. Belleview.
Burridge, J., res. cor. Pipestone and Washington.
Burridge, Jake, res. Pipestone.
Burridge, Mrs., res. Washington.
Busby, Stephen, res. cor. Bond and Centre.

Campbell, O. Mrs., res. Pipestone.
Carnahan, D. D., res. cor. Pipestone and Jefferson.
Chapman, Frank, res. Main.
Chapman, F. T., res. Territorial.
Chapman, S. R., res. Centre.
Chittenden, F. M., res. Brunson av.
Clam, Phil., res. Centre.
Clark, L. L., res. Maple.
Clark, L. L., res. Pipestone.
Colby, C., res. Pipestone.
Cole, Chauncey, res. Cherry.
Colgrove, C., res. Elm.
Collins, Geo., res. Main.

Conglon, Gardner, res. Michigan.
Conkey, I. W., res. cor. Elm and Pipestone.
Corteney, Chas., res. cor. Main and 4th.
Crowell, A. H., res. cor. Main and 6th.

Dabberthein, C. H., res. Centre.
Daily, Chas., res. Main.
Darche, J. H., res. Britian av.
David, R. J., res. Michigan.
Davis, E. M., res. Belleview.
Delong, Cynthia, res. Town Line.
Diamond, H., res. Michigan.
Donaldson, Mrs., res. Territorial.
Drury, Wm., res. Seventh.
Dunning, I. R., M. D., res. Main.

Eaker, A. J., res. Lincoln.
Easelhaurte, H., res. cor. Boughton and Town Line.
Edwards, Wm., res. Washington.
Edwards, Wm. H., res. Main.
Eldredge, B. B., res. Pipestone.
Ells, Chas., res. High.
Farnum, M., res. cor. Territorial and N. Water.
Felts, John, res. cor. Territorial and 5th.
Ferguson, Wm., res. Territorial.
Fleming, J. Mrs., res. cor. Main and 5th.
Fonger, H., res. cor. Oak and Town Line.
Fonger, Ralph, res. Pipestone.
Fowler, Levi, res. Sixth.
Fuller, M. Mrs. res. Elm.

Garhart, Wm., res. Town Line.
Gates, J. C., res. Main.
Gentle, Saml., res. Michigan.
Geronde, Herrman, res. cor. Lake and Centre.
Gibson, D., res. Territorial.
Gilson, John, res. cor. Oak and Town Line.
Gowans, Harrison, res. cor. Main and 9th.
Gowan, Wm., res. Seventh.
Graham, J. H., res. cor. Elm & Town Line.
Green, Danl., res. Town Line.

Green, John, res. Seventh.
Groom, David, res. cor. Main and Fourth.
Gummer, A., res. Pipestone.

Hacklen, M. L., res. Bond.
Hackley, L., res. Main.
Hall, C. J., res. Main.
Hall, N. B., res. Michigan.
Hall, P. Mrs., res. Elm.
Hamlin, A., res. Lincoln.
Hamlin, Charles, res. Territorial.
Hanson, P., res. Main.
Hart, A. M. Mrs., res. N. Water.
Herman, Julius, res. Territorial.
Herrman, J., res. Territorial.
Hipp, E. M. Mrs,, res. Main.
Hipp, M. G., res. Britain ave.
Hipp, Orrin, res. cor. Oak and Michigan.
Hipp, S. B., res. cor. Elm and Town Line.
Hogue, W. H., res. Brunson ave.
Holliston, L. H., res. cor. Oak and Seventh.
Hoodles. Wm., res. Main.
Hopkins, Geo., res. Belleview.
Hopkins, T., res. Elm.
Hoyt, Darius T., res. Elm.
Hudson, Elmer, res. Town Line.
Hulburt, O. Mrs., res. Main.
Hull, Saml., res. Park.
Hunt, M., res. Pipestone.
Hurlbut, Kidd, res. Washington.
Hurley, T. H., res. Main.
Hurly, Thos., res. Jefferson.

Ingham, J. C., res. cor. Britain ave. and Town Line.

Jackson, Chas. A., res. N. Water.
Jakway, E. J., res. Town Line.
James, Albert, res. Territorial.
Jaquay, G. F., res. Main.
Johnson, J. Mrs., res. Pipestone.
Johnson, J. R., res. Centre.

Johnson, Robert, res. 7th.
Johnston, Thomas, res. Main.
Jones, Mrs., res. cor. Main and 6th
Jones, R. M., res. Washington.
Jones, Wm., res. Pipestone.
Jordan, J. O., res. Pipestone.

Kelley, E. H., res. Washington.
Kidd, A. J., res. Pipestone.
Kingsley, Mrs., res. Washington.
Kinney, P. M., res. Britain ave.
Knowles, A., res. Main.
Knowles, Henry, res. cor. Territorial and 5th.
Kooms, Herbert, res Main.
Koon, M. A., res. Main.
Kyes, Chas. D., res. Jefferson.

Lamport, M. G., res. Lincoln.
Lamport, W. W., res. cor. Pipestone and Britain av.
Langley, G. D. Mrs., res. Elm.
Lauphire & Glover, 6th.
Lea, Benj., res. Territorial.
Lee, Helen Mrs., res. Territorial.
Leslie, J. W., res. Main.
Lewis, B. C. Mrs., res. Main.
Livingston, Cornelius, res. 6th.
Lynch, James, res. Park.

McCormick, I., res. N. Water.
McCormick, J., res. Territorial.
McLaughlin, John, res. cor. Territorial and 5th.
Martindale, Kellogg, res. Territorial.
Mason, J. W., res. Territorial.
Mathews, Chas., res. Territorial.
Miller, G. D., res. Pipestone.
Miller, H. W., res. cor. Jefferson and Lincoln.
Miller, J., res. cor. 6th and Territorial.
Miller, J. F., res. 1st.
Mills, ——, res. Elm.
Modic, T. J., res. Pipestone.
Montey, Hiram, res. Territorial.

Moodir, T. J., res. Pipestone.
Moore, Daniel, res. Pipestone.
Moore, Geo. B., res. Territorial.
Moore, Geo. W., res. Territorial.
Morrill, Chas., res. Pipestone.
Morrison, John, res. Main.
Morrow, Frank, res. Main.
Morrow, Monroe, res. Main.
Morton, H. C. Hon., res. Territorial.
Murphy, John, res. 6th.
Myrick, C. R., res. High.
Newell, E. F., res. Park.
Newhouse, J., res. Territorial.
Newland, Wm., res. Pipestone.
Nichols, Frank, res. Centre.
Noe, E. N., res. Main.
Nutting, O. O., res. Belleview.
Olmstead, A., res. High.
Orcutt, F. D., res. n. Water.
Oshannessy, J. J., res. Maple.
Owen, Geo. W., res. American House.
Palmer, Jay J., res. Colfax House.
Partman, Horner, res. Britain ave.
Peaslee, Chas. L., res. Territorial.
Pender, James, res. Town Line.
Pernell, James, res. 7th.
Peterson, Anna Mrs., res. Main.
Petrie, Henry, res. Michigan.
Petrie, H. E. res. Michigan.
Pierson, Mrs., res. Center.
Pike, J. C., res. n. w. cor. Main and Pipestone.
Pitcher, Henry L., res. Pipestone.
Plummer, A., res. N. Water.
Pointer, James, res. cor. Broadway and Empire.
Prescott, Phil., res. 7th.
Price, John R., res. Pipestone.
Pulsifer, Mrs., res. Lincoln.
Quilliam, Ed., res. Main.
Race, C. Mrs., res. Territorial.

Ratkoski & Tieson, Territorial.
Reis, M. F., res. Elm.
Ricaby, Geo., res. Main.
Ricaby, R., Town Line.
Rice, F. E. Mrs., res. Pipestone.
Rice, F. G., res. Main.
Riford, A. B., res. Elm.
Rittenhouse, E. M. Mrs., res. Territorial.
Robbins, Addie Miss, res. Main.
Robbins, N., res. Main.
Rounds, Geo., res. 6th.
Rowe, A. H., res. cor. Oak and Town Line.
Rowe, Jasper O., res. Pipestone.
Rowe, Mrs., res. Michigan.
Ruggs, H. W., res. Cherry.
Russell, J., res. Pipestone.
Russell, J., res. Main.
Rutter, Thos., res. Broadway.

Salzman, C. Mrs., res. Main.
Sandford, Ross, res. N. Water.
Sanverain, Ada, res. cor. Lake and Centre.
Sanverain, Ama, res. cor. Lake and Center.
Sanverain, Maria, res. cor. Lake and Center·
Scanlon, Mrs., res. Territorial.
Schans, Henry, res. Lincoln.
Schirer, John, res. 5th.
Schultz, B., res. Centre.
Scott, Chas. C., res. Broadway.
Scott, Jas., res. Territorial.
Scott, John A., res. Sixth.
Season, James, res. Elm.
Segar, Nicholas, res. Territorial.
Sheanean, Geo., res. Michigan.
Sheppard, Orrin, res. Broadway.
Sherman, F. R., res. Main.
Shultz, R. F., res. Main.
Silvers, James, res. Fourth.
Simons, A. E., res. cor. Oak and 8th.
Simons, Henry, res. Centre.

Small, John, res. Territorial.
Smith, L., res. N. Water.
Sonner, G. F., res. Lincoln.
Southworth, Herbert, res. cor. Main and 6th.
Spaulding, Fred, res. Town Line.
Spaulding, F. E., res. Main.
Spiers, F., res. Oak.
Sponsel, V., res. cor. Main and 6th.
Starks, Lewis, res. Territorial.
Stevens, James, res. cor. Pipestone and Washington.
Stevens, R. S., res. cor. Main and 6th.
Stewart, S., res. Oak.
Stoddard, John, res. Territorial.
Stuppelbean, G. G., res. High.

Taff, A. H., res, Main.
Taggart, Charles, res. Territorial.
Tarbell, Chas., res. Pipestone.
Teetzel, C. W., res. N. Water.
Teetzel, John, res. Lincoln.
Thomas, John, res. Main.
Thompson, A. H., res. Main.
Thompson, Chas. res. Territorial.
Thompson, Mr. Rev., res. Britian ave.
Thorburn, John, res. Centre.
Thresher, J. P., res. Territorial.
Tillotson, Chas., res. Fourth.
Torrance, L. Mrs., res. Pipsstone.
Troy, James, res. N. Water.
Trumbull, E. D., res. cor. Territorial and n. Water.

Valentine, G. M., res. Pipestone.
Van Arman, Sophia Mrs., res. Territorial.
Van Brackel, Fred, res. Seventh.
Vanderbeck, James, res. Elm.
Van Dusen, J. P., res. cor. Pipestone and Belleview.
Van Horn, Mrs. res. Elm.
Vincent, Alonzo, res. Main and Pipestone.
Vincent, H., res. Territorial.
Vincent, M., res. Washington.

Vincent, S. L., res. cor. Territorial and 6th.
Vinell, N., res. Fifth.
Valstak, Alfonso, res. Main.
Volsteik, A., res. Main.
Walton, James, res. Territorial.
Ward, W. C., res. Territorial.
Warner, Chas. res. Town Line.
Warner, Sylvester, res. Oak.
Weimer, J. W., res. cor. Elm and Brunson.
Wells, Richard, res. cor. Territorial and 4th.
Wentworth, A. J., res. High.
Werry, Joe, res. Centre.
Wervey, Charles, res. cor. Territorial and 4th.
White, S. M. Dr., res. High.
Willey, O. S., res. Belleview.
Williams, Geo., res. Boughton.
Williams, Henry, res. cor. Elm and Pipestone.
Williams, G. S., res. Elm.
Wilson, John, res. Michigan
Wilson, Mrs., res. Main.
Wing, A., res. Bond.
Wise, Leonard, res. Main.
Woodard, P. G., res. Main.
Woodard, W. J., res. Pipestone.
Worden, R. M., res. Sixth.
Worth, Chas. B., res. Oak.
Wright, Geo., res. n. Water.
Wright, J., res. Pipestone.
Wright, L., res. cor. Boughton and Town Line.

M. L. McCLAVE,
NURSERY

Fruit and Ornamental Trees, and Small Fruits and Grape Vines,

One mile S. E. on Pipestone Road.   Benton Harbor, Mich.

ROLLINS PUBLISHING COMPANY'S

Classified Business Directory

OF

BENTON HARBOR.

Adams C. E. meat market, Water nr. Main.
Adams John & Co., groceries, provisions, etc., s. s. Main bet. Pipestone and 6th.
Alden Evaporating Canning Co., cor. Town Line and Lake.
American Express Co., M. G. Lamport agent, n. s. Main w. of Pipestone.
American House, Alonzo Vincent propr., s. w. cor. Main and Pipestone. (See advt.)
Anchor Line of Steamers, H. F. Heath, agent, cor. Main and Pipestone.
Antisdale & Wiley, fruit growers and dealers in groceries, provisions, etc., s. s. Main w. Pipestone.
Arnt Chas., groceries, s. s. Territorial.
Austin S. M. & Co., groceries, e. s. Pipestone nr. Elm.
Baushke Theo. J., blacksmithing, carriage and wagon mfr., s. e. cor. Main and 8th.
Baute Henry, boot and shoemaker, n. s. Main.
Baute John & Son, Benton Harbor foundry and machine shop, manfrs. plows and kettles, bet. Red Warehouse and Depot.
Bell John, physician and surgeon, s. e. cor. Main and Pipestone.
Benton Harbor Excelsior Mfg. Co., H. W. Miller, manager.
Benton Harbor Mills, flour, W. E. Bradley, propr., cor. Town Line and Lake.

Benton Harbor *Palladium* (weekly), Chas. E. Reeves, publisher, Gates & Bell's block, cor. Main and Pipestone.
Black R. Mrs., dressmaker, s. s. Main.
Boyle C. S., groceries and provisions, n. s. Main.
Bradley W. E., propr. Benton Harbor Mills, cor. Town Line and Lake.
Brammall E., tinsmith and dealer in reapers, n. s. Main.
Brown Wells, notary public, fire and life insurance agent and justice of the peace, Main.
Carpenter L. & Co., box and basket factory, factory and salesroom, Main st.
Chapman Frank, picture frames, Main.
Chicago and Michigan Lake Shore Railroad, C. A. Warner agent, Benton Harbor.
Clark E. A., physician and surgeon, Rice's building, Main.
Clark L. L., groceries, e. s. Pipestone nr. Elm.
Coates A., photographer, Riford's Block, Water.
Colby C. & Co., berry boxes, peach and grape baskets, etc., Main.
Colfax House, cor. Colfax av. and Territorial, S. L. Vincent prop.
Conkey I. W., groceries and crockery cor. Pipestone and Elm.
Crowell A. H., millinery, staple and fancy dry goods, s. w. cor. Main and 6th.
Cunard Line of Mail Steamers, H. F. Heath agent, s. e. Main and Pipestone.
David R. J. & Co., dry goods, hats caps and clothing, s. s. Main.
Dunning I. R., physician, s. s. Main w. Pipestone.
Eastman John A., attorney, collections and dealer in lands, Brunsun & Johnson's Block, Main.
Edwards Will H., groceries, provisions, etc., Edwards' brick block.
Eldridge & Robbins, dealers in all kinds of lumber and contractors and builders, s. cor. Main and 9th.
Terry & Co., dry goods and clothing, 33 Main.
Fisher F. W., manager J. O. Rowe bakery and restaurant, e. s. Pipestone bet. Main and Elm.
Fonger & Stewart, propr. Gartley House, Water, nr. depot and dock.
Gartley House, Fonger & Stewart props., Water, nr. depot and dock. (See advt.)
Gates I. C., druggist, bookseller and stationer, Gates & Bell's Block, Main.

Gentle S., cooper, Main.
Godfrey Victor, saloon and billiards, s. s. Territorial.
Graham J. H. & Co., mfrs. and dealers in lumber, nr. depot.
Graham, Morton & Co., owners and proprs. Steamer Messenger and docks.
Hall C. J., dentist, s. e. cor. Main and Pipestone.
Hanson P., merchant tailor, Main.
Hurt Ann M. Mrs. restaurant, water.
Heath H. F., agt. Anchor and Cunard Line Steamers, s. e. cor. Main and Pipestone.
Herrman Julius, merchant tailor, e. s. Pipestone s. Main.
Higman, Heth & Co., bankers, s. e. cor. Main and Pipestone.
Hipp E. M. Mrs, dry goods, millinery, ladies' furnishing goods, etc., Robbins' Block, Main.
Hipp S. B., blacksmith, Town Line.
Hoodles William, saloon, Main.
Hubbard Mrs. O., millinery, ladies' furnishing and fancy goods, Main.
Hull Samuel, groceries and crockery, Main.
Ingham, Leslie & Co., mfrs. fruit packages, baskets, etc., nr. depot C. & M. L. S. R. R. (See advt.)
Jackson, Chas. A., cigars and tobacconist, Water nr. Postoffice.
Kidd, A. J., druggist, druggists' sundries, paints, oils and wall paper, Main w. Pipestone.
Kinney, P. M., groceries and provisions, Main.
Kolman Bros., news depot, Postoffice, Water.
Koon, M. A. Mrs., millinery, Main w. Pipestone.
Kyes, Chas. D., furniture and upholsterer, e. s. Pipestone s. Main.
Lampert, M. G., hardware, n. s. Main.
Langley, George Mrs., livery. C. H. Stoddard, manager, Elm.
Lanphier & Glover, blacksmiths, 6th nr. Main.
McClave, M. L., nursery, 1 mile s. e. of village. (See advt.)
McIntyre, John, painter, Pipestone.
Mills, W. H., photographer, Main.
Moodie, Thos. J., blacksmith and wagon mfr., e. s. Pipestone s. Elm.
Morrison, John, saloon, Main w. Pipestone.
Newland, Will, groceries, s. s. Main.
North Berrien County Co-Operative Association, general dealers. W. L. Hogue, business manager, n. s. Main.
Olmstead, Archer, wagon mfr., Town Line.

Orcutt, F. D., law, real estate and collecting, Riford's blk., Water.
Petrie, H. E., harness maker, s. s. Main.
Pike, J. C., saloon and billiards, Main cor. Pipestone.
Pitcher, Jones & Sonner, dry goods, carpets, clothing, gents' furnishing goods, hats and caps, oil cloths, boots and shoes, etc., Main.
Platt & Bro., hardware and agricultural implements, w. s. Pipestone bet. Main and Territorial.
Plummer, A., attorney and justice of the peace, Riford's blk.
Pointer, James, tonsorial artist, and dealer in toilet articles, collars and cigars, etc., s. s. Main.
Pointer, R. P. Mrs., ladies' hair and imitation hair goods, etc., s. s. Main.
Postoffice, A. B. Riford, postmaster, Water.
Price, J. R., druggist, e. s. Pipestone s. Main.
Red Warehouse, Graham, Morton & Co.'s dock.
Reeves, Charles E., publisher Benton Harbor *Palladium* (weekly), Gates & Bell's block.
Rice, Frank G., groceries, provisions, etc., Main.
Riford, A. B., attorney and postmaster, Water n. Main.
Rowe, J. O., meat market, e. s. Pipestone bet. Main and Elm.
Russell, J., fruit packer, s. s. Main.
Salzman, Caroline Mrs., hair dresser, Antisdale blk., Main.
Schairer & Rutkoski, grocers, bakery and restaurant, Territorial.
Schultz, R. F., trunks, and mfr. of harness, n. s. Main.
Scott & Lynch, barbers, Main.
Segan, Nicholas, saloon, s. s. Territorial.
Small, J. M., mfr. of confectionery, and Ice Cream Parlors, n. s. Main.
Smith, L., groceries, Water.
Smith & Sherno, bed springs, s. s. Main.
Spiris, Thomas, merchant tailor, Main.
Steamer "Messenger," Graham, Morton & Co., owners. (See advt.)
Talbert, Dennis, saloon, cor. Water and Territorial.
Teetzel, C. W., jeweler, Water.
Thomas, John, boot and shoe mfr., and dealer in boots, shoes, leather and findings, s. s. Main.
Trumbull & Fonger, saloon and billiard hall, cor. Water and Territorial.
Valentine, G. M., attorney, Riford's blk., Water.

Vanbrakel, Frederick, blacksmith, Town Line.
Van Dusen, J. P., boots and shoes, s. s. Main.
Vincent, Alonzo, propr. American House, s. w. cor. Main and Pipestone.
Vincent, S. L., propr. Colfax House, cor. Colfax ave. and Territorial.
Volsteck, Alphonso, planing mill, furniture mfr. and dealer, and undertaker, Main.
Warner, C. A., ticket and freight agt. C. & M. L. S. R. R.
Wenner, I. W., livery and feed stable, nr. Red Warehouse.
Wentworth Bros., mfrs. spring beds, Pipestone. (See advt.)
Western Union Telegraph Co., W. P. McDonough, manager, office R. R. depot.
White, S. M., dentist, Rice's building, Main.
Wilcox, Smith, lime, hair and cement, Main.
Wilcox, S. M. & Co., lime kiln, Territorial road bet. St. Joseph and Benton Harbor.
Williams Docks, Benton Harbor.
Williams, Henry W., mfr. and dealer in lumber, Territorial road bet. St. Joseph and Benton Harbor. (See advt.)
Winans, R., physician and surgeon, e. s. Pipestone s. Main.
Wink, John, boot and shoe maker, Main.
Woodward, P. G., dry goods, notions, etc., Main nr. 6th.
Woodward, W. J., general meat market, Main cor. Town Line.
Worden & Fonger, propr. Central Meat Market, s. s. Main.

AMERICAN HOUSE

ALONZO VINCENT, Proprietor.

THE AMERICAN is a First-Class Hotel, is located in the business center, near Postoffice, Express Office and Bank. No one will regret patronizing the American.

Satisfaction to all who Patronize.

S. W. CORNER MAIN & PIPESTONE,

BENTON HARBOR, MICH.

H. W. WILLIAMS,

Manufacturer and Wholesale and Retail Dealer in

HARD and SOFT WOOD

LUMBER.

A SPECIALTY MADE IN

Filling Bills of Ordered Lumber.

ALSO MANUFACTURER OF ALL KINDS OF

PICKETS.

Office and Mill, Territorial Road, between Benton Harbor and St. Joseph,

BENTON HARBOR, - - MICH.

ALL ORDERS PROMPTLY FILLED.

Ingham, Leslie & Co.

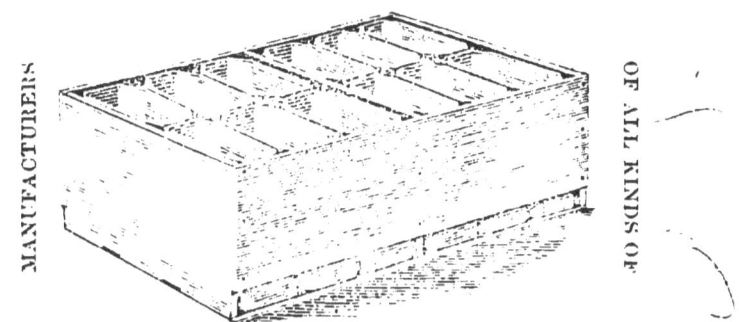

MANUFACTURERS OF ALL KINDS OF

Fruit Packages
CHEESE-BOX HOOPS,
CIGAR-BOX LUMBER

Crimped Elm Head-Linings,

VENEERS, ETC.,

Benton Harbor, - - Mich.

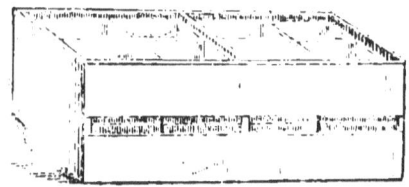

A. J. WENTWORTH.   H. S. WENTWORTH

WENTWORTH BROS.
MANUFACTURERS OF

Wentworth's Centennial Bed Spring.

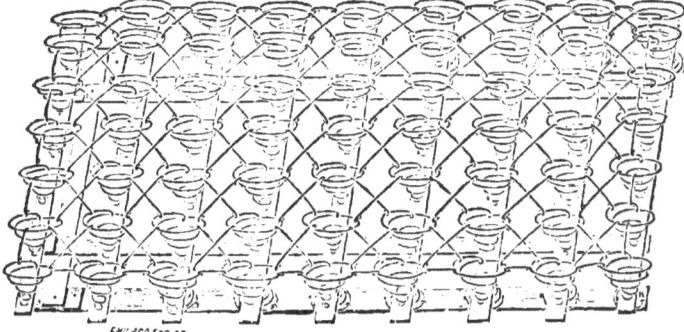

(Patented August 29th, 1876.)

The best and cheapest bed in the market. Wholesale and retail. State and county rights on reasonable terms.

BENTON HARBOR, MICH. | Factories | **DECATUR, ILLINOIS.**

GARTLEY HOUSE,

FONGER & STEWART, Proprietors.

The Gartley is a new house, nicely furnished throughout, is the only First-Class Hotel in town, is located near the post-office, steamboat dock and depot.

The proprietors aim is to keep a hotel which will attract commercial men and the traveling public on its own merits.

Water St., near Steamboat Docks,

BENTON HARBOR,   MICHIGAN

The Favorite, Elegant and fast Passenger Steamer,

MESSENGER

WILL LEAVE

BENTON HARBOR

FOR

CHICAGO

carrying freight and passengers daily, Saturdays excepted, at 9 P. M. returning leaves Chicago daily, Saturdays and Sundays excepted, at 10 A. M.. On Saturdays leaves Chicago at 11:30 P. M., thus affording parties to enjoy a whole day in the wonderful city of Chicago, visiting the theatres and returning home Sunday morning, after enjoying a good night's rest. There is no better way of spending a day than to to take this trip across the lake. Fare, berth included, $2; for the round trip $1.50 each way. Freight as low as by any other line, until June 1. The MESSENGER makes only three trips a week leaving Benton Harbor Monday, Wednesday and Friday nights at 9 P. M.

This is the best route to and from Chicago from the following points: Hager, Riverside, Colona, Watervleit, Hartford, Bangor, Breedsville, Grand Junction, Millburg, Pipestone, Eau Claire, Berrien Center, Shanghai.

GRAHAM, MORTON & CO.,

Benton Harbor, Mich, and 48 River Street, Chicago.

FRUIT GROWERS AND SHIPPERS

OF

BENTON HARBOR.

Abbey D.
Adams C. E.
Adams John.
Adams W. H. S.
Akwright J.
Alden H.
Alden Jason.
Alden J. B.
Alden P. P.
Ames Emery.
Anable E.
Anable W.
Annable E.
Annable W.
Antis C. J.
Antis H.
Anthony Jno.
Antisdale S. G.
Antisdale & Willey.
Archer Henry.
Arms E.
Arndt Chas.
Arny B.
Aspel Jas.

Aylesworth J.
Austin E.
Austin S. M.
Badgley A. N.
Baker A.
Baker Jno.
Baker L
Baker Lafe.
Baldwin O. A.
Banter G. A.
Banter G. H.
Barker H. L.
Barnard R. B.
Barnard S. J.
Barnes Peter.
Barnum A. J.
Barrows Jno.
Barry D.
Barry D. S.
Barry J. S.
Barry T. F.
Bartels H. W.
Bartholomew E.
Bartholomew Mrs.
Bartram F.

Baushke A.
Baushke C.
Baushke Chas.
Bauskhe D.
Bauskhe Gus.
Baushke J.
Beuskhe John
Baushke J. C.
Beach J. L.
Becht C.
Beck M.
Beect Jno.
Beleger H.
Bell J.
Berton R. P.
Bessy L.
Beton John.
Bishop A. D. & O. D.
Bishop B.
Bishop S.
Bolinger Simon.
Bower John.
Bowden W.
Bowden Wm.
Boyle C. S.
Boyles & Sons.
Bradford S. F.
Bradley Milo.
Bradley Owen.
Brado F.
Bragg L. D.
Brant N.
Brant Porter E.
Bratt W. B.
Bratton M.
Brechart H.
Brizee A. M.
Brooks A.
Bryant H. F.
Bryant W. C.

Broughton R. J.
Brown D. N.
Brown F. M.
Brown G.
Brown Geo.
Brown Geo. W.
Brown J. W.
Brown O.
Brown W.
Browne Wells.
Brubaker J.
Brunson A.
Brunson Stern.
Buckley P. H.
Buckman A.
Burdick S. V.
Burdick Wm.
Burdick W. S.
Burridge J.
Burridge J. N.
Burtran F. Mrs.
Burry Jno. D.
Burtzbach Philipp.
Burtzloff Chas.
Buyers John.
Calkins A. H.
Callwell J.
Calwell J.
Campbell John.
Canfield A.
Canfield B.
Canfield & Gould.
Canfield L. Mrs.
Canfield & Walroth.
Canfield Wm.
Carmichel A. C.
Carmichel B. P.
Carmichel L. P.
Cary Wm.

Castle N.
Cassidy R. & W. H.
Chadwick H.
Chadwick I. W.
Chadwick L.
Chandler M.
Chapman S. R.
Chester A.
Chester Andrew.
Chester H.
Chevens Jno.
Chivis A. B.
Church G. W.
Clark G. H.
Clark Jno.
Clarke G. H.
Clarke J.
Clarke T.
Clapsaddle P. P.
Clapsaddle Wm.
Clinton H.
Clinton H. Mrs.
Classon G. W.
Classon J. D.
Cluff C. E.
Colburn C. W.
Cole L.
Cole P.
Collins A. M.
Collins Frank.
Congdon G.
Congdon J.
Connell B. O.
Cook & Eaman.
Cook William.
Cornell L.
Cowles F. B.
Crawford J. S.
Crittenden L. C.

Crofoot D. W.
Crofoot W. D.
Crooks G. G.
Crossman D. C.
Crowell A. H.
Crowfoot W. D.
Culow W. D.
Culver P.
Cunningham E. H.
Cunningham J. M.
Curtis C.
Curtis L. H.
Cuthbert Geo.
Cutler M. M.
Daley Peter.
Dalley P.
David R. J.
Day G. W.
Day Jas.
Darche J. H.
Deaner S.
Deitle F.
Deitle Frank.
Denner Jno.
Deorduff G.
Deorduff J.
Derrduff G. W.
Dickenson J.
Dickinson J. A.
Dix D. O.
Donlen P. M.
Dorsey P. J.
Doty J. W.
Dorstewitz August.
Dorstewitz Gus.
Dorstewitz G.
Doxsee N.
Dresser A.
Dresser A. M.

Dresser R. M.
Dukesherer F.
Dukeshere H.
Dukeshire F.
Dukeshire John
Dunham Job
Dunham Jno. H.
Dunkerly G. R.
Dunkerly T. R.
Dunkleberry J. W.
Duval G. G.
Duvall M. J.
Eadus H.
Eamon F. M.
Eaman J. M.
Earls Jno.
Eastman H. D.
Edenborough W.
Edick O. M.
Edwards R. S.
Ehlerding H.
Elliott C. A.
Elliott M.
Ellis Jas.
Ells J.
Elson Geo.
Elson Jas.
Eltes H. E.
Emerson M.
Emery J. D.
Emery W. G.
Ener Barty
Enos R.
Estes Jas.
Estey E. K.
Everetts C. P.
Farley Phil.
Farnum H. C.
Felair Theo.

Fellid J. J.
Fennasy E.
Finnigan F.
Filbrant J.
Fillchin Theo.
Fisher A. W.
Flood J.
Flood John
Flood J. F.
Foster & Leeds.
Foster O. N.
Fox Geo.
Freinard Gus.
Frost K. D.
Gage H. M.
Gammer William
Garland H.
Garland H. W.
Garrett J.
Garrett Jno.
Garrison Wm.
Gates C. W.
Gates W.
Gates William
George W. L.
Gibney T.
Gibney Thos.
Gilbert C. Mrs.
Gilbert D.
Gilbert G. M.
Glade M.
Gleason C.
Godfrey C. H.
Godfrey H.
Godfrey H. W.
Godfrey V. F.
Goulette Mrs.
Gonnear S.
Goodrich M. E.

Goodsell D. B.
Grady M.
Granger F.
Granville Geo.
Granville G. F.
Grass D.
Gray J. W.
Green B.
Green D.
Green E. V.
Green M. A.
Greenfield J.
Greenfield John
Grey D.
Griswold G.
Gross D.
Gross R. A.
Grow R.
Guy D.
Guy Dewett
Guy Dewitt C.
Guy G. M.
Hadlow James
Haide M.
Hagerman T. C.
Hall W. B.
Hamlin D. H.
Hancock R.
Handy S.
Harkness P. S.
Harmon J. B.
Harnur O.
Harrington M. A.
Harris Samuel
Harrison Geo.
Hart O.
Harvey Jas.
Harvey J. E.
Haskins A.

Haskin J. F.
Haskins M.
Hathaway H. J.
Hawkins Almeron
Hawkins C. B.
Heath S. F.
Heiler Chas.
Herbert P.
Herbert Philip
Hern J.
Herrington M. A.
Hersey Rosa Mrs.
Hess J.
Hickey Jno.
Higbee James F.
Hill G. B.
Hill M. J.
Hill W. H.
Hills M. J.
Hilton H.
Hipp B. G.
Hoag E. A. Mrs.
Hogue A. E.
Hogue R. M.
Holziner F.
Hoover Geo.
Hopkins A.
Hoppe L.
Hoppy Lawrence
Houghton D.
Houghton N.
Howard Farley
Howard J. B.
Howard J. D.
Hudson Wm.
Huffman G. F.
Hughes A.
Hughs S. R.
Hull Chas.

Hull M.
Hull S. & Co.
Hull Samuel & Co.
Hurd D.
Hurd E. L.
Hurlbard O. Mrs.
Hutt M.
Ingham, Leslie & Co.
Ives A.
Ivory N.
Jackson J. C.
Jakway J. H.
James A.
Jeffrey W. Z.
Jenkens J. M.
Jennings M. A.
Jewett E. B.
Johnson A. E.
Johnson Byron
Johnson B. F.
Johnson C. E.
Johnson Francis
Johnson J. L.
Johnson L. J.
Johnson R. M.
Johnson Thos.
Johnston A. E. Mrs.
Joiner C.
Jones D. D.
Kaicher Jacob
Keller W. H.
Kelley J. H.
Kelly L.
Kennedy H. M.
Kennedy M.
Kennedy N. G.
Kenell Frank
Kenney L.
Kennell P.

Kepler N.
Kettle S. S.
Kibler C. H.
Killen Mary
Kindle P.
King A. Mrs.
King A. M.
King D.
King Geo.
King Jobe Mrs.
King R. J.
King V.
Kingsland E. L.
Kingsley L. F.
Kinney E.
Kinney P. M.
Kinney Thos.
Knizely A. J.
Kinzman E.
Kniebes Frank
Knuth A. Mrs.
Kochel Stephen
Kranse Adam
Lake G.
Lampert M. G.
Lampher E.
Landen M. V.
Lanpher E.
Lapham D.
Lavell J. P.
Lawrence D. T.
Lawrence H.
Lee James
Leintner O.
Lentz J.
Leslie J. W.
Letson O.
Linir J. C.
Linz John

Lobough H. R.
Lord G. W.
Lord Jno.
Lough Wm.
Love M.
Lovell J. P.
Lovell M. V.
Lovell N. V.
Lyons Thos.
McAllister J. W.
McCabe E.
McClare Ed. & Co.
McClave Kittie Miss
McClave M. M.
McClure T. J.
McCrone F.
McCrone Thos.
McCormick M.
McDeavmen S. H.
McDeamond S. H.
McGinnis N.
McGoulerick J.
McIntyre J.
McIntyre J. L.
McKean Lea
McKinley F. A.
McLove M. M.
McNamee Wm.
Mackey E. G.
Mackinzie J. P.
Malony A. J.
Maltby W.
Mansfield J. Dr.
Marr Reuben
Marger J. A.
Martin F.
Martindale J.
Martindale John
Martindale W.

Martindale William
Matraw M. G.
Matraw M. W.
Maxon J. P.
Mead O. E.
Mellish F.
Monte Lewis
Morrell O.
Morrell P.
Merrifield W. H.
Merrill W. H.
Merrills G. E.
Merry H.
Merry E. P.
Miller A.
Miller Bros.
Miller J. F.
Miller W.
Mitchell F. C.
Mitchell R. H.
Mitchell W. C.
Moas C.
Monks J.
Montey Lewis
Moore E. D.
Moore G. W.
Moore M.
Morrell O.
Morley F.
Morrison J.
Mortlock J. S.
Morton H. C.
Mosher J. H.
Mott A. J. Mrs.
Moulton L. G.
Much G. W.
Much M. W.
Murphy D.
Murphy Catherine

Murphy Louis
Murphy P.
Murphy Thos.
Nash J. V.
Nelson A. J.
Nelson Chas.
Nichols F.
Nichols Milo
Nichols R.
Nickerson E.
Nickerson L. B.
Noe H.
Noe W. C.
Norton A. D.
Nott D. M.
Nott W. J.
Nott W. J. & D. M.
Nowlan A. R.
Oden J. R.
Oehlhaffen J.
Ogden S.
Olds W. S.
Olmstead A.
Osborn Jno.
Osburn J.
Osborn N. H.
Owen A. C.
Park S.
Parker R. D.
Parker S. G.
Parsons A.
Pearl G.
Pearl L. M.
Pearsal A.
Peaslee C.
Peaslee C. L.
Perring J. C.
Perry T.
Peters Fred.
Peters G. H.
Peters G. M.
Peters G. W.
Peters J. H.
Peters W.
Peterson A.
Pfaff W.
Pfler Theo.
Phaff W.
Pierce R. T.
Pike Wm.
Piper John
Piper Wm.
Pitcher Perry
Plumb S.
Plummer A.
Pomeroy G. W.
Pratt W. B.
Prayne W. F.
Prillwitz T.
Pullin F.
Purdy C. C.
Purdy C. G.
Rabel J.
Ragatz J. H.
Raterbough D.
Rathburn D.
Reasor J. H.
Rector D. S.
Rector Wm.
Regatz J. H.
Rembolt Samuel
Remington D.
Ricird Mary
Rice F. G.
Richards J.
Richards Joseph
Rickard Mary Mrs.
Riford A. B.

Ripley F.
Ripley T. J.
Roan Chas.
Roberts Jacob
Roberts Jas.
Roberts L. H.
Robertson G. A.
Robertson G. H.
Robertson R.
Rockwood C. D.
Rogers Samuel
Rogers Sylvester
Rose J. W.
Rounds C. B. F.
Rowe W. S.
Rowley L. A.
Ruggles L. M.
Ruggles L. W.
Runyan C. V.
Runyan O. V.
Russell J.
Russell Philo.
Ryan James.
Ryan P.
Schever Chas.
Schever Peter.
Schick F.
Schmuhl H.
Schnell J. L.
Schultz B.
Scofield E. B.
Scott S. C.
Seal Henry.
Seel J. J.
Seal Phil.
Seeley M.
Seger A.
Seiber Joseph.
Sepola M.

Silvers Jas.
Silvers Jerry.
Sink H.
Shank S.
Shankland V. A.
Sheldon A. F.
Sheldon H. A.
Sherer D.
Sherman Wm.
Shever John.
Sherwood C. H.
Sherwood I.
Sherwood J. S.
Shiniman Geo.
Shiver W. H.
Shlanker A.
Shoap Saml.
Shouse Jacob.
Shultz B.
Slanker A.
Slater Geo.
Smalley M. M.
Smalley M. M. Mrs.
Smith B.
Smith Burt.
Smith Ed. L.
Smith Elijah.
Smith Ezra.
Smith G.
Smith G. I.
Smith Jno.
Smith J. P.
Smith Levi.
Smith Sebastian.
Smith W. H.
Smith W. R.
Sonner G. F.
Sorter J. E.
Southerland B. W.

Southworth A.
Southworth S. Mrs.
Spencer C. A.
Spencer Wm.
Spink E.
Spink J. M.
Spink R.
Stauffer J. B.
Stanley R.
Stanley S.
Stark H. M.
Stark L. E.
Starks H.
Starks L.
Stein C.
Stein P. V.
Stonecliff D.
Sterling John.
Stevenson W. J.
Stewart J. F.
Stiles A. F.
Stone J. R. Col.
Strese F.
Stresser F.
Stroam J.
Stump J. H.
Stupplebean G. G.
Sinvan J.
Sutton C. C.
Sutton L. F.
Sweet W.
Swisher J. H.
Swisher Josiah.
Swisher L. H.
Taber Ernest.
Tabor R. F.
Tallwitz F.
Taylor L.
Taylor O. D.

Terry T. A.
Terry T. M.
Teelzel G. W.
Tibbs A. J.
Thayer R. C.
Thomas D.
Thompson A. H.
Thornburn J.
Thresher J. P.
Tool G. N.
Todd J. F.
Tonken J.
Tracy L.
Troy L.
Trumble E.
Trumbull G. W.
Tnyon L. F.
Tubbs A.
Tubbs H.
Tupper F. E.
Tyler P. S.
Tylor S.
Vanbranken D.
Vanderbeck C. A.
Vanderburg J. M.
Van Dyne Sam.
Vanlone L.
VanPatten A.
Vanranken D.
Vaughn. D. S.
Versaw T. E.
Versaw J. P.
Vogle L.
Wade F.
Wade F. S.
Wakely W. H.
Walker F.
Walker H.
Walker T. A.

Walker T. H.
Walkins R. D.
Walrath F. D.
Ward A. J.
Ward L.
Ward L. M.
Ward Thos.
Warner C. A.
Walson J. H.
Weaver Jno.
Webb A. C.
Webb J. R.
Webber Jacob.
Webster A. Mrs.
Webster H. H.
Webster H. Mrs.
Webster M. M.
Webster R. L.
Weckler J.
Weed E.
Wees Wm.
Weimer J. W.
Welcher E. C.
Westfall Julius.
Westphall Jno.
White H. F.
White J. A.
White J. H.
Wickler J.
Wickwire W.
Wier S. W.
Wilcox S. M.
Willett E.
Williams C. A.
Williams C. P.
Willming G.
Wilming G.
Wilson Geo.
Wilson W. J.
Winans L. M.
Winans R. Dr.
Winslow C. B.
Wisner J. F.
Withey J.
Withey J. G.
Withey W. F.
Wooley Israel.
Wooley J.
Woodruff Asof.
Woodruff Jno.
Woodward G. W.
Woodward W. J.
Worthington B.
Wright G. W.
Yarrington E.
Yerrington M. C.
Yoar M.
Yoar Otto.
Yore Matt.
Yore Michael.
Yore Patrick.
York Patrick.
Yore Peter.
Young Casper.
Youngs S.
Yund P.
Yund P. & A.
Zimmerman W. C.

FRUIT GROWERS AND SHIPPERS
OF
ST. JOSEPH.

Abbe A. G.
Allen Robt.
Archer F.
Ashoff H.
Baker H.
Barlow A. P.
Barnes T.
Batcheler B. W.
Beach H. G.
Bean J. A.
Bear J.
Benning D.
Berg J.
Berg S.
Beyea Wm.
Birdsay A.
Birkholm E.
Bole J.
Botham T. H.
Bowerman P.
Boyer E.
Brain Edward
Brown C.
Brown G. A.

Burford S.
Burkey V.
Burns E. D.
Buzek J.
Canavan J. A.
Canfield M.
Carlton A. H.
Carpenter L.
Chrest J.
Christ B.
Collins Mrs. L. J.
Corkey A. H.
Cornings G. F.
Cornings S. H.
Crane C. F.
Crane O. F.
Critchfield A.
Cromer C. L.
Cromer Geo.
Curtis A.
Curtis C.
Deamer E.
Donaldson J. A.
Edwards E. M.

Egert H.
Eggert H.
Ensley W. G.
Ensley H. G.
Evans H.
Ewald F.
Farley D.
Fikes J.
Finnigan J.
Fonda G.
Freund J. B.
French A. O.
Gand J. T.
Garlinger W.
Gast F.
Geisler C.
Gnerwock C.
Gobiel P.
Godoun A. M.
Gould N. P.
Graham J. W.
Greiffendouf C.
Gruhner J.
Gurmsey H. C.
Halliday A.
Ham Peter
Happ G. F.
Hasse A.
Henry R.
Heyer J. E. C.
Hoffman F.
Hudson Wm.
Hutchinson G.
Huxley S.
Ingram J.
Jacobs E. A.
Jasper F.
Jenson P.
Johnson W.

Knuth L.
Kapson C.
Kinsley R. N.
Lambrecht J.
Langley J. H.
Langley S. G. Mrs.
Lee J. H.
Leonard M. H. Mrs.
Leute J.
Littleton W.
Lyon W. R.
McGuigan J. E.
McMaster A. H.
McMaster G.
Maitland D.
Mason F.
Mathews W. L.
Matkes Bauer
Maxon J. P.
Medinger P.
Meinitz S.
Meyer B. J.
Meyers David
Meyers Thos. S.
Milke W. G.
Miller C.
Miller N.
Miller Wm.
Miller Willis
Mischke Wm.
Moore G.
Moots W. A.
Mundt Wm.
Murphy John
Murphy J. T.
Norton D.
Osborn O. B.
Olson O.
Owen Kate

Palmer E. C.
Parker R. D.
Paschke L.
Patzkasky A.
Pekoffska M.
Peoples W.
Pennell W.
Perkins E. B.
Perry F.
Peters W, F.
Phelps C. P.
Philebrandt A.
Phillips P. B. Mrs.
Pike W.
Pixley B. F.
Prierbe A.
Race J.
Ransom F. T.
Rea Wm.
Regatz O.
Rhemen G.
Riley J. H.
Ripley C. F.
Roberts Dr.
Roe A. S.
Roe E. J. Mrs.
Rofe T. S.
Rogge C.
Ross D.
Ross M. E.
Rumsey S. E.
Runo C.
Runo J.
Rowley A. D.
Sauerbier C.
Sauerbier F.
Schaub Wm.
Schneider W.
Scott A. H.
Scott C. H.
Scott G. M.
Scott J. P.
Seasongath A.
Seavin Anna
Shaw S. Mrs.
Shepard M. & A.

Simpson Wm.
Smith E.
Smith W. B.
Snyder J.
Spading C.
Spellman M.
Spenser B.
Spry Wm.
Stahl W.
Stett J.
Sterns J. E.
Stevens Eri.
Sunday J. H.
Sutherland J. B.
Sweet O. M.
Tate R. C.
Tansch L.
Thompson M. J. Mrs.
Trenberg J.
Truhn J.
Vale E. S. B. & Co.
Van Brunt R.
Vanderpool A.
Van Dusen P.
Van Every M.
Vossell J.
Wadsworth S. P.
Walker A.
Wallace John
Walbrath W. H.
Wasco W.
Waters W.
Webb J. R.
Webber P.
Webster J. D.
Wheaton Col.
White M. A. Mrs.
Whittlesey J.
Williams B.
Wilson J. E.
Wilson J. H.
Winchester A. O.
Wissing Wm.
Yund A.
Zebbell C.
Zinzom F.

BERRIEN SPRINGS.

Bachtel Wm.
Boon Bros.
Brook D. W.
Brosins P.
Brinn J.
Clark H.
Cowen J.
Cullerton J.
Davis N. J.
De Field J.
Desten J.
Dower J.
Dougherty F.
Dudley L. E.
Edson G.
Essick A.
Feather D. T.
Fether E. A.
Feather J. H.
Feather F.
Flisher A.
Frank P.
Garr A. L.
Gohl H.
Gray F.
Green J. A.
Hall C. A.
Harner A. M.
Hartlein M.
Horner W. H.
Howe H. D.
Hull Dr.

Ireland E. M.
Kephart J.
Kimmel G. H.
Koon A.
Kugle J.
Lemon A.
Lemon M. J.
Lord D.
Lord S. J.
McNar E. A.
Mathews R.
Moyer H.
Parse L. F.
Pullen C. B.
Radtka A.
Rocky G. C.
Ross J. R.
Sermon E.
Shroyer J.
Spoon H. A.
Stemm A. K.
Steiner John
Stevick L.
Stover J. H.
Stowe S.
Summers P.
Weed J.
Weedman G. F.
Whitestone J.
Williams M.
Winfield B.
Wire A.

ROYALTON.

Abraham C.
Archer Leroy
Beamis F.
Bemis L.

Bert J. E.
Briney E.
Brooks S. O.
Christiansen H.

ROYALTON---Continued.

Colyer R. D.
Daley P.
Danforth E.
Fisher J.
Fogle G.
Franklin A.
Guyotte J.
Hankins J. M.
Haskins A.
Heime F.
Heime J.
Hess H. C. Mrs.
Kentner M.
Johnson L. K.
Long A.
Madison H.
Mayhew S.
Merwin G. W.
Miltenberger G. W.

Murphy J. T.
Nasson G.
Penland H. J.
Pew Thos.
Porter S. W.
Renfrew H.
Ross J.
Roneger O.
Sander J.
Scofield H. L.
Small A.
Smoke C. S.
Spry S. R.
Stewart M. A.
Suin A.
Tryon W. H.
Versaw W.
Vove M.
Weed J.

BAINBRIDGE.

Andrews G. S.
Arndt D.
Arndt Frank
Arndt Jacob
Arny Benedict
Bolinger S.
Buchback Philip
Burbang H. G.
Burnett W. J.
Clarke Jno.
Classen J. D.
Cribbs J.
Eber Jasper
Edinborough R. C.
Elges W.
Ernsberger D.

Gray Wm.
Gustin W.
Guy D.
Hoesbine Martin
Howard R. S.
Kaiser J.
Kesler Philip
Kisler Phil.
Kreiger Jno. C.
Lambsen O.
McCabe Mrs. E.
McGoldrich J.
McKeller D.
Matraw M. G.
Much Geo.
Remington D.

BAINBRIDGE---Continued.

Seel J. J.
Sterling J.
Stiles A. F.
Watkins R. D.
Westfall R.
Wise Chas.
Woodruff Asof
Yund P.

MILLBURG.

Adams A. D.
Adams Ed.
Anklee V.
Austin E.
Bishop J. K.
Blakeslee Wm.
Chappell C. B.
Dunham Vina
Enos R.
Fryer P. J.
Haid M.
Haid Richard
Haide Kayes
Hayd Kayes
Hess G. W.
Kameron J.
Miller J. F.
Morrill O.
Morrison D. J.
Mosher Chas.
Norton A. D.
Persoll Wm.
Piersall W.
Potis C. C.
Rackliff H. A.
Russell L. Mrs.
Weber John
Wilcox Amos
Wilder Geo.
Wilder Wm.
Woodruff H. A.
Yund P. H.
Zeglemun Peter

COLOMA.

Banken J. H.
Beck Michael
Boyer D.
Bratton M.
Bunker J.
Carter C.
Carter E.
Grey C. E.
Hughs Alfred
Ingraham E.
Jeffrey W. Z.
Jans D. D.
Jones J. H.
Miller A.
Mott Theo.
Osgood B. F.
Seber Jas.
Seger Hamilton
Williams J.
Worden J. E.

STEVENSVILLE.

Baley & Bro.
Brown G. W.
Brown W. W.
Brush A. E.
Collins E. D.
Corrigan J.
Cowell A.
Keen A. J.
Keler F. A.
Knight D.
McCoy W. A.
McDaniels A.
Owen A. C.
Percell J. N.
Putnam A. L.
Schomcksor Wm.
Singer P.
Slight J. B.
Wagner J.

TRANSIENT.

Ankatell R.
Buckman Geo.
Cassidy R. & W. H.
Ganoe Geo.
Gardner L. D.
Griswold Guy
Howell B. K.
Kreiger Peter
Rice N.
Scott Daniel
Ward S. D.

HAGAR.

Burrows C. H.
Farley P.
Gates C. W.
Gonsolus B. C.
Hess J.
Merrill E.
Noe Jno.
Sorler J. E.
Woods H. H.

SODUS.

Fisher J.
Flasher F.
Gano H.
King F. F.
King J. E.
King M. F.
King W. L.
Sharai W. F.
Tubber W.

RIVERSIDE.

Beech Jno.
Bishop A. H.
Bishop A. S.
Cole H. H.
Cutler Solan
Gallager Geo.
Safford S.

MISCELLANEOUS.

McAllister C. Mrs., Pipestone.
McDonald J. S., Pipestone.
Rector David, Pipestone.
Flewallen J. W., Dowagiac.
Flewelling D. B., Dowagiac.
Wrist J., Dowagiac.
First Fred., EauClaire.
Fisher Josephine, EauClaire.
Rosevelt O. V., Keeler.
Scott C. S., Keeler.
Liffler Vincent, Hartford.
Hendricks N., Decatur.

BERG & McCANN,

COMMERCIAL

161 LaSalle Street,

CHICAGO.

www.ingramcontent.com/pod-product-compliance
Lightning Source LLC
Chambersburg PA
CBHW022116160426
43197CB00009B/1043